PYTHON

MACHINE

LEARNING

A Comprehensive Beginners Guide to Learn Python Machine Learning from A-Z

TABLE OF CONTENTS

Introduction 1

Simple elegant syntax... 1

It is not so strict 2

The language is expressive 2

Community and Support 3

Chapter One: Why start with Python when Machine learning? 4

Supervised Learning 6

Unsupervised Learning.. 6

Step 1: Brush up your math skills........................... 6

Familiarize yourself with linear algebra for data analysis......... 7

Mathematical analysis.. 7

Gradient descent 7

Step 2: Learn the basics of Python syntax............. 8

Step 3: Find out about the main data analysis libraries................. 8

Step 4: Come up with structured projects 10

Step 5: Work on your projects 10

Why You Should Use Python.................................... 11

Readability and maintainable code...................... 11

Multiple programming paradigms 11

Compatible with a number of platforms and systems........... 12

Robust standard Library 12

Access open source Frameworks and tools 13

Simplification of complex software development 13

Adoptive to test-driven development 14

Chapter Two: Functions in Python **15**

Built-in functions 15

User-defined functions 16

Anonymous functions 16

Function and Methods 16

Parameters and Arguments 17

How do you define a function? 18

User-defined Functions (UDFs) 18

The return statement 19

How do you add Docstrings to a Python function? 22

Function arguments in Python 23

1.Default arguments 23

2.Required arguments 23

3.Keyword arguments 24

4.Variable number arguments 25

Global and Local Variables 26

Chapter Three: The Basics of Machine learning **27**

What is the Difference between Machine Learning and Artificial intelligence? 27

Building blocks of Machine Learning 29

Data 30

Model 30

Objective function 31

Optimization algorithm 31

Supervised and Unsupervised Machine Learning 32

Supervised Learning 32

Unsupervised Learning 34

Semi-supervised learning 35

Understanding Python Versions................................ 35

What of Package Manager? 38

How to install pyenv... 39
    Building dependencies 39
    Using the pyenv-installer..................................... 40

Using pyenv to install Python.................................. 42

How do you use your new Python? 43

How Does Python work? 45

Chapter Four: Step-by-Step guide on How to Install Python..........49

Why is it important to understand the difference in versions?.... 49
    Python 2.. 49
    Python 3.. 50
    Python 2.7... 50

So, what are the key differences? 51

Installing Python on Windows.................................. 53
    Step 1: Download Installation Files 53
    Step 2: Preparing Installation 55
    Step 3: Complete and verify the python installation 55

Installing Python on Mac... 55
    Step 1: Install Xcode 55
    Step 2: Install Homebrew 56
    Step 3: Install Python 3.. 57

Python Virtual Environment..................................... 58

Linux System 59
    Step 1: Check Python version and update package manager. 59
    Step 2: Installing Python 3 on Linux Mint and Ubuntu 59
    Step 3: Installing Python 3 IDLE............................. 60

Setting Up Environment Variables.................................... 60

Setting up PATH in Windows 61

Setting PATH in Mac and Linux 65

    Step 1 66

    Step 2 66

    Step 3 66

Installing PIP... 66

    Managing python packages with PIP 70

Chapter Five: Running Python on your device 71

    Installing Python on Windows 71

    Verifying Python Installation....................................72

    Configure your Python installation 73

    Set the environmental variables..............................73

    Running Python on Windows 74

    Run Python Using Command Prompt in Windows 74

    Run Python Script as a File.....................................75

    Running Python on a Mac..75

    Installing Python on a Mac......................................76

    Initiate the Terminal 76

    Install Python 77

    Install GIT 77

    Run a Python Script on a Mac or Linux 77

Chapter Six: How to organize the Python Code.............. 79

    Python Keywords 79

    Naming Identifiers 79

    Rules for Writing Identifiers....................................80

    Exploring Variables...81

    Recognizing Different Types of Variables 82

Working with Variables in this Language 83

The None Variable 85

Writing Comments in YourCode.. 87

Working with Operators.. 89

Comparison and Relational Operators............................... 92

Assignment Operators.. 93

The Functions in Python 94

Calling a Function 94

Chapter Seven: Mastering Data Preparation with Python..............97

Step 1: Preparing for the Preparation 98

Step 2: Exploratory Data Analysis 98

Step 3: Dealing with Missing Values................................. 100

Step 4: Dealing with Outliers.. 102

Step 5: Dealing with Imbalanced Data 103

    1.Using the right evaluation metrics 104

    2.Resampling the training set....................................... 104

    3.Using K-fold cross-validation the right way 105

    4.Ensemble various resampled datasets........................ 106

    5.Resample with various ratios 107

    6.Clustering the abundant class 108

    7.Designing own models 108

Step 6: Data Transformations.. 109

Step 7: Finishing Touches & Moving Ahead 110

Chapter Eight: Data Preprocessing with Machine Learning 112

Getting the data set.. 113

Importing the libraries that you need 114

Importing the data that you need 115

Handling any missing values that show up............................ 117

Handling any of our categorical data...................................... 118

Scaling the data we have 120

Chapter Nine: Linear Regression with Python.....................123

Linear regression when we just have one variable 123

Importing the right libraries.. 123

Importing the Dataset 124

Analyzing the data 124

Going back to data pre-processing 125

How to train the algorithm and get it to make some predictions
.... 126

Chapter Ten: Tips to Make Machine Learning Work for You 129

Tip #1 Remember the Logistics.. 129

Tip #2 Mind the Data 130

Tip #3 Algorithms Are Not Always Right................................... 131

Tip #4 Pick out a diverse *toolset* 133

Tip #5 Try Out Some Hybrid Learning....................................... 133

Tip #6 Remember That Cheap Doesn't Mean That Something Is
Bad 135

Tip #7 Never try to call it AI 136

Tip #8 Try Out A Few Different Algorithms................................ 136

Conclusion...139

Introduction

Have you been thinking of learning Python as your first programming language? Do you have data that you have generated and do not know where to start analyzing them? Are you interested in digesting your big data into meaningful information that will inform decision makers? Well, you have come to the right place!

Machine learning is a subject that has quickly become popular in a wide range of domains such as Data Science, Artificial intelligence among others. The use of machine learning in these domains offers incredible opportunities. If you are just starting your career, this could just be the best decision you make.

So many people think that they need to have expertise in math and programming for them to use Python at all. Trust me, you need zero-experience! All you need is interest and a strong motivation to learn all these things. You may be thinking to yourself "But why Python?" Well, there are so many reasons why Python is the best programming language to start with. Some of these reasons include;

Simple elegant syntax

One good thing with using Python is that it is so much fun! The fun in it comes because of its ease in writing codes and understanding them. This is mainly because the syntax feels so much natural and you can tell it whatever you want.

For instance;

I can simply tell it

a= 6

g=5

sum = a + g

print (sum)

By just looking at this script, you can already tell that the program adds numbers and prints them. You do not need programming knowledge to know that!

It is not so strict

Unlike other programming languages like R, python does not need you to define the type of variable you are using. As a matter of fact, at the end of each statement, you do not need to add semicolons. However, one thing that you have to bear in mind is that python follows sets of good practices such as proper indentation. The good thing with this is that it makes learning quite seamless especially if you are a beginner.

The language is expressive

By expressive, we simply mean that python allows you to write and hence you can achieve a greater degree of functionality with just a few lines of codes. It has a user-friendly graphical interface and truth is, you will be amazed at how much you can actually achieve with python once you have mastered all the basics.

Community and Support

Python has so many users across the world and this means that there is a large supporting community that you can make use of. With so many online forums available, you can reach out to them with questions and dilemmas you face while learning Python and they will help you with tough situations! Some of these forums include; Learn python subreddit, Python questions-stack overflow among others.

That said, if you are a beginner, and do not really know where to start Machine Learning with Python, then keep reading to learn more. This book contains all the great information and resources that you can make use of so that you not only gain knowledge into the basics of python, but also solve problems and accomplish projects and tasks you have at hand.

So, what are you still waiting for? Let us dive right in and get started!

Chapter One

Why start with Python when Machine learning?

Well, it is simple! If your main aim is to grow into a successful coder. We are not saying that others that started with other programming languages are not successful. However, for Machine Learning and Data Science, python is the simplest of them all because it is very easy to master and use with confidence.

When you are looking into having a future in machine learning, it is critical that you select the right coding language from the onset. It is your choice that will determine your future. While on this step, it is critical that you make your priorities right by strategically thinking so that you do not end up spending too much time on things that are not necessary at all.

In our opinion, python is the perfect choice for a beginner. This is because of the reasons we have already discussed above, but also to help you focus on selecting the right field in data science and machine learning. Additionally, you will realize that this programming language is essentially minimalistic and intuitive with a well-established framework that helps reduce the time needed to get results. Let us look into the steps that you need to understand as far as Machine Learning process is concerned.

Brief overview of Machine learning process

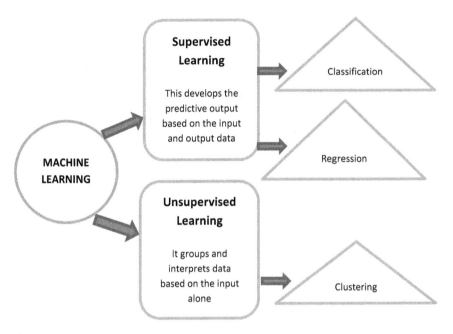

It is important to note that machine learning is learning on experience. For instance, if you are learning chase, you probably will learn first by watching others play. Similarly, a computer can be programmed by providing it with information that will train it so that it acquires the ability to identify various elements or features with a high degree of confidence.

Some of the stages that you will need to know as far as machine learning goes include data collection, sorting, analysis, development of algorithms, checking the generated algorithm, and eventually using that algorithm to draw conclusions. In order for you to look for patterns, it is critical that you use various algorithms. These algorithms are divided into two; supervised and unsupervised learning.

Supervised Learning

When it comes to supervised learning, it simply means that the computer is able to recognize various elements based on the samples provided. In other words, once you feed the data to a computer, it will study it and develop an ability to recognize it.

For example, you can simply train your computer to recognize spam messages and automatically filter them based on information that you have received previously. Some examples of supervised learning algorithms include; decision trees, Naïve Bayes classifier, k-nearest neighbors, support-vector machines and linear regression among others.

Unsupervised Learning

Unlike the supervised learning we have touched on earlier, unsupervised learning implies that the machine receives a set of input data only. At this point, the main role of the machine is to determine the relationship between the data that has been keyed in and other hypothetical data. Here, the machine is not provided with a set of verification data. Instead, the computer itself has a role to play in finding a pattern(s) and the relationship between various datasets. Hence, the unsupervised data is classified into two major groups; association and clustering.

Step 1: Brush up your math skills

You do not have to be a math guru to do machine learning. However, you have to have basic mathematics skills. Otherwise, you will not be able to deal with machine learning or data science projects without basic knowledge of math. The trick is for you to devote at least 30 minutes each day to brush up your skills in math so that it becomes effortless when it comes to learning advanced topics in Python. There is no point in taking a whole class in math, all you need to know are the key concepts, period!

So, how then can you learn math?

Familiarize yourself with linear algebra for data analysis

These include such concepts as matrices, scalars, tensors and vectors. For instance, the principal component method requires that you understand the eigenvectors. On the other hand, when it comes to regression, you need to know multiplication of matrices. This is mainly because machine learning often uses high-dimensional datasets with so many variables and this data is best represented in the form of matrices.

Mathematical analysis

These include such concepts as derivatives and gradients. One important thing to bear in mind is that mathematical analysis is a critical element when it comes to machine learning algorithms. In this case, derivatives and gradients play a central role in problems that require optimization. For instance, gradient descent is a common optimization method.

Gradient descent

This is important when it comes to building basic neural networks right from scratch. One of the best ways in which one can learn math is to try and use linear algebra to serve as your network and then use mathematical analysis for optimization. Particularly, you will create a gradient descent right from scratch. You should not worry too much about the nuances of the neural network, the secret is to try as much as possible to follow the instructions and develop a code for it.

Step 2: Learn the basics of Python syntax

Well, python and analysis of data are not synonymous and so you do not have to worry too much about getting a full learning course. To minimize your chances of failing, it is critical that you learn by simply swimming technique. When you are in a swimming class, learn your Python syntax in parallel and you will be amazed how effective this skill is at gaining deeper insight.

The truth is, it is not worthwhile to just study syntax for the sake of it because this increases the risk of losing interest. Additionally, it is not necessary to memorize everything. The point is to ensure that you are taking baby steps in combining theoretical knowledge with practice. Pay attention to the intuitive understanding of how operators work. This way, you will slowly grasp the syntax through reading the documentation and in the process of writing your own codes. Before you know it, you will not be writing codes anymore.

Step 3: Find out about the main data analysis libraries

The other step is for you to revise so that you can mug up the Python section that is only applicable to data science. As mentioned earlier, it is indeed true that python has a vast number of libraries. Libraries simply refer to a collection of in-built functions and objects that you can easily import into your environment so that you spend less time writing a script from scratch.

This is how you use your libraries. Simply open your Jupyter notebook and then go over the library documentation. This will take you 30 minutes to an hour to complete. Then import the library into your Jupyter Notebook. After importing, ensure that you follow all the steps on your guide to ensure that the library is functioning well.

You can explore the documentation to determine what else it can do. Well, this is just to let you know how to use the library. However, at this point, we do not recommend learning libraries because there is a high likelihood that you will have forgotten everything or most of it by the time you begin implementing them in projects. The best thing is for you to find out what each library can do.

Apart from Jupyter Notebook, you can also use others like Numerical Python (NumPy). It is universal and quite versatile for both newbies and pros in programming. When you use NumPy, you are definitely going to operate an array of matrices with so much ease. They also have a number of useful functions like linear algebra and numerical conversion operators.

You could also use Pandas, which is a high-performance tool for presentation of data frames. The good thing with it is that you can import data from any source, create new parameters, calculate a number of functions, and build queries. The other advantage of using Panda is the fact that it has numerous matrix transformation functions including sliding window methods for purposes of getting information from the data.

Finally, you could also use Matplotlib which a rather flexible library that plays a critical role in creating visualizations. However, in spite of the fact that it is powerful, it is tailor-made for power users. Therefore, as a beginner, you can choose to skip it and use the others we have mentioned to get started. Once you have mastered the basics, then you can try using Matplotlib.

Step 4: Come up with structured projects

Once you have mastered the basics of python syntax and libraries, it is high time that you start creating projects. The good thing with creating projects to work on, you will be exposed to a different kind of challenge that allows you to learn new things. It will also help you create a portfolio for future job searches.

Step 5: Work on your projects

There are so many projects that are available and you can work on. however, as a beginner, it is critical that you work on projects that stir up passion from deep inside you. when you start working on your own projects, you get to learn a lot of things and handle challenges perfectly well. This is important especially if you are aspiring to land a job in machine learning fields and taking on more challenging projects.

There are so many reference materials that you can use to help you figure out certain challenges. Some of these resources include; Python documentation which is one of the best reference materials when you are learning python from scratch. StackOverflow is another multi-functional site that has a bunch of questions and possible solutions that people discuss. One thing that helped me so much while learning python was such forums.

I believe that the problem or challenge that you face when learning or handling various aspects of your project is not unique to you alone. There are many other programmers out there that have encountered a similar problem and somehow found a way to solve it. In other words, when you go to such forums as GitHub, you will get suggestions and many solutions to unstuck you! With GitHub, you also have access to projects that people have done in the past within your field that you can follow so that you know what to expect when handling your own.

Why You Should Use Python

So, I know that we have already discussed why python is the best programming language to begin with. However, there are several other factors that make python a go-to programming language as far as machine learning is concerned. These factors include;

Readability and maintainable code

When writing a software application, one thing that you have to pay attention to is the quality of the source code. This goes a long way in simplifying maintenance and the process of updating. In python, the syntax rule permits you to express various concepts without necessarily having to write new code.

At the same time, unlike other programming languages, Python emphasizes on the readability of codes and you can use English keywords rather than using punctuations. In other words, you can create custom applications with Python without having to write any additional codes. It is the readable and clean code base that plays a significant role in updating and maintaining the software with no extra effort and time spent.

Multiple programming paradigms

Just like other programming languages, python supports a vast array of programming paradigms too. It fully supports both structured and object-oriented programming. Additionally, its language features offer support to quite a number of functional and aspect-oriented programming concepts. It also features a system that is both dynamic and automated in terms of management of memory. This way, you can use python to develop large and complex applications to perform various tasks.

Compatible with a number of platforms and systems

Currently, python offers support to a wide range of operating systems. You can simply use Python interpreter to run a number of codes on certain tools and platforms. Alternatively, you can run the same codes on several platforms without necessarily having to recompile them. Once you make alterations on the code, you do not have to recompile them once again. This means that once you make changes to the code, you can run it and check the results immediately. It is because of its features that you can easily make changes to the code without having to increase the time of development.

Robust standard Library

One of the things that make Python quite powerful is the robust standard library it has that no other programming language has. It is this standard library that plays a critical role in allowing you to select from a large array of modules based on what your precise requirements are. Additionally, each of the modules allows you to add functionality to python application without having to write more code.

For instance, when you write a web application in Python, you could use particular modules for implementation of web services, management of operating system interface, performing a string of operations, as well as work with internet protocols. You can also gather a lot of information about various modules by simply scanning through the Python library documentation.

Access open source Frameworks and tools

This is an open source programming language that unlike other paid software, will help you significantly cut down on cost. You can also choose from a vast array of open source python frameworks and tools based on your needs.

For instance, to speed up the development of web applications, you can choose to use a more robust Python web framework. Such frameworks include; Flask, Bottle, Django, Cherrypy, and Pyramid. Additionally, you can speed up the development of a desktop Graphical user interface application using Python GUI frameworks.

Simplification of complex software development

Because python is a general-purpose language, you can simply use it when developing both web and desktop applications. You can also use python in developing much more complex scientific and numeric software applications. It is designed with features that play a significant role in data analysis and visualization.

The good news is that you can leverage the data analysis features in creating custom data solutions for "Big Data" without necessarily having to put in more time and effort. It also provides APIs and visualization libraries that play a role in visualizing and presenting data in a more appealing way for ease of understanding. So many developers today use Python for processing tasks for natural data and Artificial Intelligence.

Adoptive to test-driven development

Python is very important in the fast creation of prototypes for various software applications. You can also build software applications directly from the prototypes. All you have to do is to refactor the Python code initially used in the prototype. It also makes it easier for you to do coding at the same time as testing it by simply adopting a test-driven development approach.

With Python, you can easily write a test before you can write down the code and then use the tests to evaluate the continuous application of the code. This test can also serve as a checkpoint of the application meets certain predefined criteria with reference to the source code.

However, one thing that you have to bear in mind as far as python is concerned is that unlike other programming languages, it has a number of shortcomings. It lacks some built-in features that are offered by the modern programming languages like R programming. This means that you have to ensure to use Python libraries, frameworks and modules to speed up the custom software development.

According to so many studies, Python is a little slower compared to other programming languages such as C++ and Java. The secret is for you to make changes to the application code as fast as you can by simply using the custom runtime. However, you can always use Python to fast track the software development process while simplifying its maintenance.

Chapter Two

Functions in Python

In order for you to perform a set of tasks or instructions that you would like to use repeatedly, it is important that you have functions in programming that will help you achieve just that! The secret is to bundle them up because they are quite complex and are better off when they are self-contained in a sub-program. This means that when you need them to perform a given task, you just call them.

So, really what is a function? Well, you can define a function as a piece of code that is created with the aim of carrying out a specific task. In order to carry out that task, the function may need an input, and in other cases, this is not necessary. Once the task is achieved, the function can return certain values.

In Python, there are three types of functions that you will be working with to achieve a set of tasks. These are;

Built-in functions

These functions include; **help()** that you use to ask for help. It contains information about a certain function and what it is supposed to do; **min()** that you can call to get a minimum value from a certain string of values; **print()** that plays a role in printing out an object to the terminal. You can also find more of these functions here.

User-defined functions

Also denoted as UDFs. They are functions that you use to help you out.

Anonymous functions

This is also referred to as lambda functions. This is mainly because they are not declared with a standard **def** keyword.

Function and Methods

So many people wonder whether there is a difference between a method and a function. Well, a method simply refers to a function that is part of a class. In other words, you access it with an object of a certain class. However, functions do not have to have these kinds of restrictions. It simply refers to a standalone function. In short, all methods are functions, but not all functions are methods!

Let us consider this example where you have to first define the function **plus()** and then summation class using the method **sum()**

```
#Define a function 'plus()'
def plus (a,g):
 return a + g


#Create a 'Summation' class
class Summation(object):
 def sum(self, a, g):
  self.content = a + g
return self.content

Run
```

On the other hand, if you would like to call the **sum()** method, this is part of the **summation** class, it is important that you first define an instance of that particular class. This is how you can define such an instance;

16

```
Instantiate `Summation` class to call `sum()`
 sumInstance = Summation()
  sumInstance.sum(1,2)
Run
```

One thing that you have to bear in mind is that this instantiation is not necessary when you are calling the **plus()** function. All you have to do is execute **plus(1,2)** without any problem.

Parameters and Arguments

When you are defining a method or a function, you use parameters as names, and this is what arguments will be mapped onto. This means that, arguments are those things supplied to any function or method call. In other words, method/function code refer to arguments by means of parameter names.

Let us consider the example above where you pass two arguments to **sum()** method belonging to the **summation** class. Previously we have defined three parameters that include; **self, a,** and **b.**

So, what happened to **self?**

Well, the very first argument of every class method serves as a reference to the current object of that class. In this case, it is the **summation**. Conventionally, the argument in this case is **self**. This means that you do not pass the reference to self mainly because self is a parameter name for an argument implicitly passed. For which it serves as an object by which a method is called. In other words, it is implicitly inserted into the argument list.

How do you define a function?

There are four major steps that you define a function in Python. These steps include;

1. Using the keyword **def** to declare the function. Then follow that up with a function name.

2. Secondly, add parameters to the function. Ensure that the parameters are within the parenthesis of the function. Then complete that line with a full colon.

3. Thirdly, add a statement(s) that define what the function is required to execute.

4. Finally, complete your function with a statement **return** is the function is required to give an output. You have to understand that without the return statement, the output you get will be **None.**

For example

```
def hello():
    print("Hello Mummy")
    return
Run
```

As we dive deeper into Python functions, you will realize that they will become more complex. You will be adding loops, flow control and many other things to make them fine-grained.

For instance;

```
def hello ():
name = str (input("Enter your name: "))
if name:
  print ("Hello " + str(name))
else:
  print ("Hello Mummy")
return
hello ()
```

In this example, what you are doing is asking the user to key in their name. If the name is given, then the output will be "Hello Mummy", otherwise the response will be a personalized "Hello". Additionally, you can define more than one function for your UDF. We will delve deeper into this when we discuss the function and argument section. The other thing that you have to remember is that you can or cannot return multiple values from your function.

The return statement

It is important that you understand that while printing something in your UDF such as **hello ()**, you do not necessarily have to return it. this is because there will not be a difference between the function we have written above and the one below.

```
def hello_noreturn():
  print("Hello Mummy")
Run
```

In some instances, you may want to continue with the output you get from your function to try other operations. In this case, you will have to use the return statement to return a value. It could be a string, integer or any other type of output.

Let us consider the following example where the function **hello()** returns a string "**hello**". On the other hand, the function **hello-noreturn()** returns the output **None**.

```
def hello():
 print("Hello Mummy")
 return("hello")
def hello_noreturn():
 print("Hello Mummy")
```

Then multiply the output you get from the first function by five. So,

```
Hello() * 5
Run
On the other hand, try to multiply the output you get from the second
function by the same value as the first. So,
Hello-noreturn() * 5
Run
```

What do you get? Well, you will get an error on the second function mainly because you cannot perform an operation with a **None** output. You simply get a **TypeError** which simply means that you cannot do multiplication on this kind of input.

What you have to bear in mind in this case is that a function will immediately exit when it comes across a return statement, even in cases where it will not return a value of any kind.

```
def run():
    for x in range(10):
        if x == 2:
            return
    print("Run!")
run()
Run
```

The other thing that you have to understand is that when you are
working with the return statement, you can make use of it to return
several values. To achieve this, simply use tuples. What you have to
bear in mind is that this data structure is quite similar to a list because
it can have multiple values.

However, tuples are immutable. This simply means that you cannot
modify anything that is stored within it. You can just construct it with
the use of double parentheses. To unpack the tuple into several
variables, you can make use of comma and an assignment operator.

For example;

```
# Define `plus()`
def plus(a,g):
    sum = a + g
    return (sum, a)
# Call `plus()` and unpack variables
sum, a = plus(6,10)
# Print `sum()`
print(sum)
Run
```

What you have to note is that the return statement **return sum, a** will
have a similar result as the function **return (sum, a).** what is
interesting is that the former function actually packs **sum** and **a** into
one tuple!

How do you call a function?

In the sections we have discussed above, there are so many examples that we have seen that involves calling a function. Therefore, calling a function simply refers to you executing the function that you have already defined, whether directly using the Python prompt, or using another function. To call our newly defined function hello(), you simply execute as below;

```
hello()
Run
```

How do you add Docstrings to a Python function?

The other important part of writing a Python function is the docstring. The role of the docstring is to describe what the function you define does. This could be computation or returning values. It is these descriptions that serve as documentation for your functions such that when anyone reads the function's docstrings, they get an insight into what the function does. The good thing is that with docstrings, you will not have to trace through all the codes in the definition of functions.

Once you have written your function header, you can place the function docstring in the line after. It should be in between triple quotations. For instance, for the function hello(), the right docstring would be 'Prints "Hello Mummy"'

One thing that you have to note is that the docstrings may be prolonged. Therefore, if you would like to dig deeper into more details of docstrings, there are Python Libraries on GitHub like pandas where you can access more examples.

Function arguments in Python

We have already discussed the difference between parameters and arguments earlier. Therefore, you now know that arguments are things given to a function or method. On the other hand, the function or method code simply refers to arguments based on the name of the parameters. There are four major types of arguments that UDFs can take in Python. These are; default arguments, required arguments, keyword arguments, and variable number arguments.

1. Default arguments

Just as the name suggests, these are arguments that take a default value in case there is no argument value passed when you call a function. This simply means that you can assign a default value by the assignment operator =. For example;

```
# Define `plus()` function
def plus(a, g = 2):
  return a + g

# Call `plus()` with only `a` parameter
plus(a=6)
# Call `plus()` with `a` and `b` parameters
plus(a=6, b=10)
Run
```

2. Required arguments

Just as the name suggests, the required arguments refer to those that must be there. They are simply arguments that need to be passed when you call a function and has to be in a precise order as in the function below;

```
# Define `plus()` with required arguments
def plus(a, g):
   return a + g
Run
```

What you simply need in this case are arguments that will map to **a** and **g** parameters so that you can call a function without running into an error. If you decide to switch around these two parameters, the outcome will not be different. However, it will change if you alter the function plus() to the following;

```
# Define `plus()` with a required argument
def plus(a, g):
   return a/g
Run
```

3. Keyword arguments

The keyword argument plays a critical role in Python in the sense that it allows you to call all the right parameters in the right order. They are simply used in identifying arguments by the name of their parameter.

For instance;

```
# Define `plus()` function
def plus(a, g):
   return a + g

# Call `plus()` function using the parameters
plus(6,9)
# Call `plus()` function using the keyword arguments
plus(a=5, g=8)
Run
```

When using a keyword parameter, you can play around with the order of parameters but still get similar results after executing the function intended.

```
# Define `plus()` function
def plus(a, g):
  return a + g

# Call `plus()` function with keyword arguments
plus(a=5, g=11)
Run
```

4. Variable number arguments

In case you do not have an idea on the number of arguments you would like to pass to a certain function, it is possible to achieve results using the syntax ***args** as below;

```
# Define `plus()` function to accept a variable number of arguments
def plus(*args):
  return sum(args)
# Calculate the sum
plus(1,4,5)
Run
```

One thing that you have to note is that the asterisk comes before the name of the variable holding the values of the non-keyword variable arguments. You might also pass such arguments as ***var args int** among others to the **plus()** function. The trick is ensuring that you place the ***args** with an alternative name as long as it has an asterisk and the code will still work.

Additionally, you will realize that the function above uses built-in functions like **sum()** in summing all the arguments that you pass to the **plus()** function. However, if you choose to avoid this entirely so that you build your function from scratch, this alternative will work as well.

```
# Define `plus()` function so that it can accept multiple number of arguments

def plus(*args):
    total = 0
    for i in args:
        total += i
    return total
# Calculate the sum
Plus (30,60,90,50)
Run
```

Global and Local Variables

As a general rule, those variables that are defined inside a function have a local scope, while those defined outside possess a global scope. In other words, local variables lie within a function block. They also are accessible within that very function. On the other hand, global variables refer to those that can be obtained by all functions within your script.

```
# Global variable `init`

init = 1
# Define `plus()` function to allow a variable number argument
def plus(*args):
    # Local variable `sum()`
    total = 0
    for i in args:
        total += i
    return total

# To access the global variable
print("this is the initialized value " + str (init))
# (Try to) access the local variable
print("this is the sum " + str (total))
Run
```

When you run the script above, you will get a **NameError**. This simply means that the name total is not defined when you print out the local variable **total** which was initially defined within the function body. On the other hand, the **init** variable is printed out without a problem.

26

Chapter Three

The Basics of Machine learning

What is the Difference between Machine Learning and Artificial intelligence?

So many people often confuse between deep learning, machine learning and Artificial intelligence. Well, what we would like you to do is think of all these as a set of Russian dolls that are all nested within one another starting from the smallest to the largest. So, deep learning is a subset of machine learning. That said, machine learning is also a subset of Artificial intelligence. However, one thing that you have to note is that not all Artificial intelligence is necessarily machine learning!

So, what is Artificial Intelligence?

Well, the term AI is made up of two keywords; Artificial and Intelligence. Artificial simply refers to something that is manmade and not natural. Intelligence on the other hand simply refers to the ability to think and understand various things, concepts or phenomenon. So many people think that AI is a system.

The truth is, AI is not a system. In fact AI is actually implemented in a system. You can define AI in various ways. For instance, you can think of AI as a study of various ways of training computers to do things that humans can presently do better. In other words, AI is an intelligence where what you are simply doing is adding as many capabilities that humans have to a machine.

So, what is Machine Learning?

Well, this term refers to the learning in which a machine is capable of learning on its own without necessarily being programmed explicitly. In fact, you can think of machine learning as an application of AI that offers systems the ability to learn automatically and get to improve with experience. In this case, you can actually generate a program by simply incorporating the input and output of the program. Therefore, you can define machine learning as learning from an experience E a certain task T and then measuring the performance P of the learners. In other words, what you will be measuring is performance P as the experience of the machine in a certain task improves.

Here are the key differences between AI and ML;

Artificial Intelligence	Machine Learning
Intelligence here represents the acquisition of knowledge and ability to apply it	Machine learning simply represents an acquisition of skills to perform a task
The main aim is to increase the success rate and not necessarily accuracy	The main aim is to increase accuracy without necessarily caring about success
This works just like a computer performing a smart task	This simply involves the machine taking a dataset and learning from it
It simulates natural human intelligence for the purpose of solving complex problems	It learns from a dataset so that it can maximize its performance on a particular task

It is decision making	It is carefree in that it allows the machine to learn as many new things as possible from the data
It develops a system that mimics human response by the machine in certain situations	It is all about creating self-learning algorithms
Finds optimal solutions	Goes for any solutions, whether optimal or not
Leads to intelligence	Leads to knowledge

Building blocks of Machine Learning

Think of machine learning now as a black box in which you key in your input to the machine learning algorithm that trains itself and then produces the desired output. It is similar to training a child to do something and then they do an exam and perform well. Now, for a machine algorithm to perform what it is supposed to, there has to be a number of building blocks namely; Data, model, objective function and optimization algorithm.

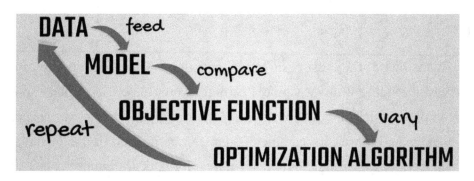

Data

One thing that you have to understand is that Machine Learning cannot be what it is supposed to be without data, and the good thing is that data is everywhere. What is interesting is that over the past decades, the work on Machine Learning shifted from being knowledge-driven to being data-driven. This is because scientists began designing computer programs for analysis of big data and then using the results to draw inferences and learn from it.

In the same manner, Machine Learning uses data from historical events to train the algorithm. The thing is from the big data you have, about two-thirds of it is used in training the ML algorithm and the remaining one-third is used in testing the purpose.

Model

Once you have determined what data you would like to train your Machine Learning Algorithm on, then it is time to feed that on the model. The model is usually an algorithm or a function. For instance,

$y = mx + b$

Where;

y = *output*, m = *input*, x = *weights*, b = *bias*

This is one of the most basic model equations. This is referred to as a Linear model. With Machine Learning, you can create much more complex models or equations to serve your purpose. On the other hand, weights and biases are parameters that can be learned in this formula. Their values are often initialized randomly and are controllable and adjustable so that you can get the desired output.

Objective function

Once the model is trained on a particular dataset, it is critical that they are compared to determine how close they are to reality. This is exactly where objective functions come in to play. In other words, objective function refers to a measure of the closeness of the model's output from the target.

Optimization algorithm

Once the objective function has checked how close or far the trained model is to the target, the next step is to correct the algorithm. The main reason for this correction is to ensure that a high level of accuracy or optimization is attained.

In other words, the optimization algorithm plays a central role in helping achieve accuracy by simply using values of the objective function and then varying the model's parameters. This is repeated over and over again until the model arrives at values of the parameters for which the objective function is absolutely optimal.

That said, Machine Learning is quite similar to the way humans learn. Normally, as a person, you have to do lots of practice that involves many mistakes before you can attain perfection in a certain task or steering a project in the right direction. In other words, there is no human that is perfect from birth.

The same applies to machines. They have to perform as much practice as possible to become perfect. It is these four building blocks that you can think of as ingredients that play a significant role in helping the ML algorithm reach its optimal stage of perfection after a lot of trials and errors.

The only difference between ML and humans is the fact that with a proper model machine and dataset, machines can learn way faster than an average person can do. This goes a long way in helping humans achieve their goals efficiently and is the reason why ML matters in the first place.

Supervised and Unsupervised Machine Learning

Within the Machine Learning field, there are two major kinds of tasks; the supervised one and the unsupervised tasks. The major distinguishing factors between the two is the fact that supervised learning is based upon ground truths. In other words, it requires prior knowledge of what the input values should be. This is mainly because the main goal here is to learn the function such that when it is given a set of data and desired output, the machine is able to determine the relationship between the two. However, with unsupervised learning, there are no labeled outputs. Therefore, the main goal is to conclude on the basis of natural structures seen within the data points.

Supervised Learning

Before we can delve deeper into what supervised learning is, one thing that you have to appreciate is that this is used in a majority of practical machine learning. Now, supervised learning refers to where you have input variables designated as x and the output variable is designated as y. Here, the algorithm is then put to task to learn the mapping function right from the input all the way to the output.

$Y = m(x)$

The main reason why this is referred to as supervised learning is that, you can think of the process of an algorithm learning from the training data as a teacher responsible for supervising the process of learning. This means that, the teacher knows the correct answer, but then the algorithm will keep giving predictions based on the training dataset. The point when the algorithm attains a level of performance that is deemed acceptable marks the end of the learning process.

There are two major groups of supervised learning problems namely; regression and classification. A regression problem refers to one in which the output variable is a real value like weight, height and dollars among others. On the other hand, classification problem refers to one in which the output variable is simply a category like diseased or not diseased, red or green among others.

Let us consider the following example. Supposing you are given a basket full of various types of fruits. The first thing to be done is to train the machine with all of them one fruit at a time. That means that, if you have an object that is rounded and has a top depression and the fruit is red in color, then that is labeled as an Apple. If the shape of the object is similar to a long curvy cylinder and is yellow-green in color it is labeled as Banana.

Now, once you have trained the data, you are offered a separate basket of fruits and then asked to identify what they are? Well, the truth is, considering that the machine already has learned these things from the input data given previously, it will use that knowledge wisely. It will classify the fruits based on shape and color and then confirm what the fruits are one by one putting them in categories. In short, what the machine is doing is learning things from training data and then applying that knowledge to the test dataset.

Unsupervised Learning

Unlike supervised learning, Unsupervised learning refers to a situation where you have only the input data and no corresponding output. The main aim of this is to model an underlying structure of data distribution that will aid in discovering more about the data.

The main reason why it is referred to as unsupervised is that in this case, there is no correct answer and there is no teacher at all. In other words, the algorithms are allowed to devise their own ways of discovering and presenting data in an interesting structure.

Unsupervised data can be grouped into two major categories namely; association and clustering. Association learning problem refers to one in which you would like to discover rules that give a description of a huge chunk of the input data like people purchasing item X and also tend to purchase item Y.   On the other hand, clustering learning problems refer to those in which you would like to discover the inherent groups within a dataset like a customer with a certain behavior of purchasing.

Let us consider the following example. Supposing you have an image with both cats and dogs that have never been seen before. In other words, the machine has no idea what features each has and cannot categorize them as either a cat or dog. However, it can place them in categories based on their say; differences, similarities and patterns. In that case, the machine will put all dogs in one class and cats in another based on the differences or similarities and yet it did not have prior information on any of them.

Semi-supervised learning

Well, now that we already know what supervised and unsupervised learning are, there is another concept that is left for us to learn; the semi-supervised learning. This simply refers to a problem where you have lots of input data with just a small proportion of the data labeled. In other words, the problem in this case is both supervised and unsupervised learning.

A very good example of this is having an image with cats, dogs and people inside and a majority of the images are not labeled what they are. One thing to note is that so many real-life machine learning problems fall into this class. This is mainly because it is costly to label all data. In most cases you require access to domain experts to do that. With unlabeled data, the cost is low and not to mention the ease that comes with collecting and storing the data.

To learn the structure of your input data, you simply use unsupervised learning techniques. On the other hand, if you want to make the best predictions for data that is unlabeled, you simply use supervised learning techniques. All you have to do is feed the data into supervised learning algorithms to serve as your training data and then use a model to make predictions on the unseen data.

Understanding Python Versions

There are so many Python versions available and every new release comes with major or slight improvements. There is a high chance that your computer already has python installed. To check if you already have it installed in your computer, simply go to **Applications** and then **Utilities** and Click **Terminal**. The short cut of this is simply pressing command-spacebar, and then typing in *terminal*. Then press **Enter**.

To find out what version of python you have installed, simply type in the command as below;

```
Appless-MacBook:~ apples$ python --version
Python 2.7.10
```

This is the version that I have on my computer. If you see something like this depending on the version you have. If you have version 3 installed, you should see something starting with say 3.4.1. Whatever version you have, if you are just getting started, it is okay if you just used the version that is already installed.

That said, there is also a chance that you can have multiple versions of python installed in your computer. Some people would love to contribute to a project that supports several python versions. Well, if you are not sure how to test all of them, do not worry because managing multiple versions has never been too easy with the use of *pyenv.*

So what is pyenv?

This term simply stands for python environment. It is a tool that is used in managing various versions of python. If you already have python installed in your computer, you may still find it useful to have pyenv installed. This will play a significant role in allowing you to try out as many new language features as you can to ultimately contribute to a project that requires many versions of Python.

You may be thinking to yourself, but then why not just use system python?

Well, system python is just the python that comes already installed on your Operating system, whether you are using Mac, Linux or windows.

This means that when you just type in Python, what you get is Python REPL. So really, why don't we just use it?

Let's look at it this way, python belongs to OS, after all that is why it came already installed. Which means that, when you type in;

```
Appless-MacBook:~ apples$ which python                          ]
/usr/bin/python
```

This simply means that the python I have is available to all users just as the location path suggests. Trust me, there is a high likelihood that this is not really the version that you want for your project. In order to install a package into your python, it is important that you run;

```
Appless-MacBook:~ apples$ sudo pip install
```

This is mainly because when you do that, you get to install Python package globally, which becomes a major problem when another user comes in and desires to install a different version from what you already have because it is password protected. In other words, you can only authorize the installation of a new package on your OS.

But, one thing that you have to understand is that when you install so many versions of the same package, there is a high chance that they will creep up on you and cause a lot of unexpected problems. One of the complains that people have is that that the package that has been stable on your system suddenly starts misbehaving and after several hours of trying to troubleshoot, you realize that you installed the wrong version.

Even though you may already have your python version /usr/local/bin/Python 3.5 for instance, you may still be not safe. You may run into similar permission issues and flexibility problems as already mentioned earlier. Additionally, you really do not have so much control over what version of python comes installed on your OS. However, if you are using Ubuntu and would love to install the latest version, then you might just be unlucky because the default version is obsolete. In other words, you might need to wait for a new OS to be released.

What of Package Manager?

This is your next option. Such programs as port, yum, brew and apt may help, after all they are the ways in which we install most packages to our OS. Unfortunately, you will face similar problems as above when using a package manager.

The truth is, package managers install their packages by default into the global system space rather than the user space. When you do this, your development environment is polluted and this makes it quite hard to share workspaces with other users.

Let us just mention again that you do not have any control over what python version comes installed on your OS. In spite of the fact that some repositories will offer you various options to choose from, by default, what you are looking at is a version your vendor has. Therefore, if you went ahead and installed Python from a package manager, imagine what would happen if you were creating a package and then you would love to test it on another version say 3.7? How would you be able to switch in between various versions? Yes, you can do it but it is much prone to errors and is quite tedious.

With all these problems in mind, let us have a recap on the right criteria to us when installing and managing Python versions with so much ease and flexibility;

1. Start by installing Python in your user space

2. Ensure that you can install multiple versions of Python as you wish

3. Ensure that you specify the exact version you want to use

4. Switch in between various installed versions

To do all these and more, pyenv is there to sort you out!

How to install pyenv

So now we have agreed that pyenv is what you need. However, before you can install it, one thing to note is that you will need a couple of OS-specific dependencies. In other words, you will need some development utilities that are written in C and are needed because to install python from pyenv, it will need to build it right from the source. Pyenv originally did not support Windows OS. However, with the advent of pyenv-win projects that were released recently, you just might be in luck if you are using windows.

Building dependencies

Pyenv program works by building python right from the source. What this means is that you will need to build dependencies for you to use pyenv. This is something that varies from one platform to another in that, if you are using Ubuntu and would like to install build dependencies, you can use the following;

```
Appless-MacBook:~ apples$ $ sudo apt-get install -y make build-essential libssl-
dev zlib1g-dev \
> libbz2-dev libreadline-dev libsqlite3-dev wget curl llvm libncurses5-dev \
> libncursesw5-dev xz-utils tk-dev libffi-dev liblzma-dev python-openssl
```

What this means is that to install all the dependencies, Apt is used. Allow it to run on your computer and you will be set for Ubuntu systems.

On the other hand, if you are using Fedora/RHEL/CentOS, you can install the build dependencies using *yum* as below;

```
Appless-MacBook:~ apples$ sudo yum install zlib-devel bzip2 bzip2-devel readline
-devel sqlite sqlite-devel openssl-devel xz xz-devel libffi-devel
```

If you are using macOS like I am, then simply type in;

```
Appless-MacBook:~ apples$ brew install openssl readline sqlite3 xz zlib
```

This particular command depends on Homebrew and you can also install that into your computer for it to work. The thing with this is that you will install just a few dependencies for macOS.

Using the pyenv-installer

Once you have installed all the dependencies, you are now set to install pyenv itself. It is recommended that you use the pyenv-installer project for that.

```
$ curl https://pyenv.run | bash
```

This will help install but a few plugins that you can use. Some of these include;

1. Pyenv which is the actual pyenv application

2. Pyenv-doctor is a plugin that is used in verifying that pyenv and build dependencies are actually installed

3. Pyenv-virtualenv is a plugin for pyenv application as well as the virtual environment

4. Pyenv-which-ext is a plugin that automatically lookup various system commands

5. Pyenv-update is a plugin that is important for updating the pyenv application to the current version

You could also download the pyenv-installer script and run it locally. This allows you to see exactly what it is that you are installing. At the end of the installation process, you should be able to see something like this;

```
WARNING: seems you still have not added 'pyenv' to the load path.

# Load pyenv automatically by adding

# the following to ~/.bashrc:

export PATH="$HOME/.pyenv/bin:$PATH"

eval "$(pyenv init -)"

eval "$(pyenv virtualenv-init -)"
```

However, one thing that you have to note is that the output often depends on your shell. The most important thing is that you follow instructions on how to add pyenv to your path such that you can easily initialize pyenv/pyenv-virtualenv auto-completion. Once this is done, it is advisable that you reload the shell by typing in;

$ exec "$SHELL" # or you can just choose to restart your terminal instead. With that done, you will have your pyenv installed and all four important plugins along with it.

Using pyenv to install Python

At this point, you already have pyenv installed and the whole point of doing that is so that you can install Python. This is our next step. As mentioned earlier, there are multiple versions of python to select from. Therefore, for you to see all the available versions, simply do this;

```
Appless-MacBook:~ apples$ pyenv install --list | grep " 3\.[678]"
```

Once you run this command, you will have all the Python versions listed for you. Once you know what versions you want and are not already installed, all you have to do is install them with just a single command;

```
$ pyenv install -v 3.7.2
/tmp/python-build.20190208022403.30568 ~
Downloading Python-3.7.2.tar.xz...
-> https://www.python.org/ftp/python/3.7.2/Python-3.7.2.tar.xz
Installing Python-3.7.2...
/tmp/python-build.20190208022403.30568/Python-3.7.2 /tmp/python-
build.20190208022403.30568 ~
[...]
Installing collected packages: setuptools, pip
Successfully installed pip-18.1 setuptools-40.6.2
Installed Python-3.7.2 to /home/realpython/.pyenv/versions/3.7.2
```

Well, don't wait up as this might take quite a while. The main reason for this is that pyenv is building Python from the source and once it is done, you will have the version that you wanted available on your machine. However, if you also do not wish to see all the output from the installation process, you simply omit the -v flag.

Once installed, you may be curious about the location of your newly installed python version. As we have repeatedly mentioned, pyenv builds python right from the source. Therefore, every single version that has been installed into your machine will be located in the pyenv root directory. All you can do to check is type the command;

```
$ ls ~/.pyenv/versions/
```

All the versions will be listed right below the command. This is something that is quite handy especially when you wish to get rid of some versions as it may be trivial. Just type;

```
$ rm -rf ~/.pyenv/versions/2.7.11.
```

The good thing with pyenv is that it offers you the command that you can use in uninstalling certain versions. For instance;

```
$ pyenv uninstall 2.7.11
```

How do you use your new Python?

Now that you have python versions you want all installed, the next thing would be to know how to use them. The first step is to check again all the versions that you have available on your OS.

```
$ pyenv versions
* system (set by /home/realpython/.pyenv/version)
```

When you run the command, all the versions available will be listed below it. The * simply indicates that the system Python version is currently active. You will also realize that it is set by a certain file in the pyenv root directory which means that by default, you are using the system Python.

```
$ python -V
Python 2.7.2
```

When you try to confirm this using which command as below, you will get the exact location of the python version that is actively being used by your computer.

```
$ which python
/home/realpython/.pyenv/shims/python
```

Are you surprised? Well, this is exactly how pyenv program works. This is because it inserts itself into your path and from your operating system's point of view when you can call it, it will be executed. To see the actual path, simply use;

```
$ pyenv which python
/usr/bin/python
```

Now, you may be wondering whether the version that you just installed is working. To get that peace of mind, all you have to do is run the built-in test suite as below;

```
$ pyenv global 3.8-dev
$ python -m test
```

What this does is that it will kickstart lots of Python's internal tests to verify your installation. At any one time when you wish to use the initial version you had, simply use the command;

```
$ pyenv global system
$ python -V
Python 2.7.2
```

With this, you can easily switch between various versions of Python with so much ease.

How Does Python work?

This is one of the questions that most beginners ask. We are all curious about what happens as soon as we hit the Enter button and the code we are running is executed on the CPU. Well, one thing that you have to understand is that python uses a code module that is interchangeable. In other words, rather than using a single long set of instructions that is standard for most programming languages, Python uses a simple code. This standard implementation of python is often referred to as cpython.

What happens is that rather than python converting its code into machine code that the hardware can understand, it simply converts it into byte code. In other words, within Python, a compilation will take place but just not in the language the machine understands. This explains the reason why there is a need for a Python virtual machine that performs the execution of the byte codes.

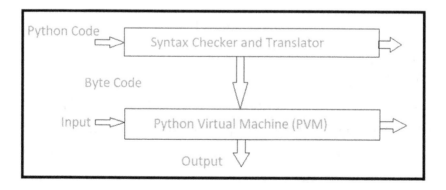

Once you run the code, it gets parsed, analyzed and then transferred into an interpreter, what is referred to in computer science as compiler theory. The main role of the compiler program is to translate the code from one language to another. Trust me, this is something that we can cover in the advanced course but for now, we will just look at the basic version for the sake of understanding.

So, the compiler starts with a parser which is a routine that plays an important role in reading the source code and then applies the syntax rule of the language to it. This is to ensure that it can determine the validity of the python code. If it does not make sense, the parser simply throws an error which causes the compiler to bail out. However, if the python code is deemed to be valid, then the parser outputs an Abstract Syntax Tree (AST).

AST is simply a tree data structure in which each of its nodes contains a parameter of the syntax. For instance if you say x = 3, there is a chance that you could end up with;

1. A binary expression node with an operator value of the '=' sign

2. A left value that refers to the reference expression 'x'

3. A right value referring to the integer literal expression '3'

In other words, your entire program can be represented using a big tree like the one above. Then it moves on to the second phase of semantic analysis. This simply means trying to figure out what AST really means. In other words, the parser will check if everything is okay and whether you did something illegal in spite of the validity of the parse. It there is an issue, then an error is raised. Otherwise, it will analyze the AST and then perform any edits to make it much simpler for the machine to understand.

The third phase will entail the generation of code. When you have fully analyzed, simplified and checked the validity of AST, it is fed to a generator that walks the AST in order to produce code in the output language, and this serves as your end product.

With python, a compiler is used instead of an interpreter. Well, the interpreter works the same way as a compiler. However, there is just one major difference between the two; instead of generating code, the interpreter will simply load the output in memory and then directly executes it on the system.

It is important to note that all but the very simplest languages are accompanied by a set of predefined functions important to so many users, and they would be hard for users to implement on their own due to a number of reasons. The code might call into the functions without necessarily requiring a third-party library. For instance, in Python the command print sends its output to stdout. The thing is, these set of functions are collected in shared libraries the code can call during runtime. This is why it is referred to as a language runtime library.

Just as a recap, there are three major roles of the Python interpreter;

1. It is the role of the Python interpreter to read the python code or set of instructions. It then verifies that the instructions have been formatted well by checking the syntax on each line. If there is an error, the translation process is immediately paused and an error message is thrown.

2. However, if there is no error, in other words the python code is well-formatted, then the python interpreter proceeds into translating it into an equivalent form referred to as the byte code, which serves as an intermediate language. Once the execution of the python code/script is successful, it is translated completely into Byte code.

3. Finally, the byte code is directed into the Python virtual machine (PVM) where it is executed. If an error occurs during the execution process, the process comes to a halt and an error message is issued.

Chapter Four

Step-by-Step guide on How to Install Python

Why is it important to understand the difference in versions?

If you are looking to get started with Python programming language as a beginner, one of the questions that you might be asking is which version I should learn- Python 2 or 3? Well, just so that we can understand and make an informed decision, it is important that we look at what each version has to offer and what features might actually sway you as a coder to one over the other.

Python 2

This is one version that became more transparent as well as inclusive through the implementation of Python Enhancement Protocol. This is something that offers information to a community of users as well as giving descriptions of new features of the language. Python 2 also offers a way one can maneuver around the changes in the black box in other languages.

With this version, there were improvements in garbage collection and allocation of memory. There was also additional support offered for Unicode to standardize its characters for global use. With this version, the users can also create a list based on already existing lists. As more features were added, there were hierarchies also created and hence 2.1,

2.2 and so on. According to statistics, over 97% of users have used some version of Python 2, indicating a strong base of its developers.

Python 3

This is the version that is currently still under development. It was released in 2008 with the main aim of addressing the design flaws of Python version 2. The main focus of this language was to clean up the codes and eliminate redundancies since the previous version had so many ways of performing a single task, hence creating so much confusion.

This version also improved the manner in which integers are handled. One thing that is important to note is that Python 2 had a wide range of package libraries available for its users, something that made version 3 less attractive to many. This made the developers stress over the fact that version 2 did not seem to have an end life and hence support was now available only through the community and not the development team. This cause python 2 users to shift to Python 3, which has currently caught up with the number of package libraries that 2 had.

Python 2.7

This was the last release of Python 2 following the release of version 3 in 2008 as mentioned earlier. The main aim of this particular version was to make it quite easy for version 3 users to migrate seamlessly by offering them some degree of compatibility between the two. This explains the reason why this version has persisted among many programmers as well as its robust libraries. Therefore, when we refer to Python 2 we are simply talking about Python 2.7 as it is widely used. However, it serves as a legacy version that will lose its official support in 2020.

So, what are the key differences?

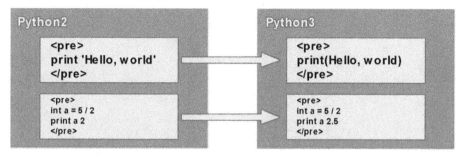

Some of the most important differences to note between the two versions include the following;

- Widely different options in their package libraries

- In Version 3, the directories lack the init.py

- There is large community support available for version 3

The most interesting thing is that much of the differences that you will encounter are mostly on their syntax. For instance, the print command has changed from a keyword to function.

print 'Hello, there'

And thus has now become;

print ('Hello, there')

There is also a slight change in the division of integers such that in Version 3 vernacular, when you divide an integer with a remainder, what you get as output is a floating point. In the past, dividing integers simply outputs an integer with no remainder.

```
Int b= 7/2
print b
3
```

Today;

```
Int b= 7/2
print b
3.5
```

To get the remainder in Python version 2.7, you have to use modulus math. Alternatively, you can add a decimal point to the values so that it is 7.0 divided by 2.0 in order for you to get the expected value 3.5.

The final difference between Python 2.7 and 3.0 is the fact that Version 2 uses ASCII characters while 3 uses Unicode characters. When you use Unicode characters in Python 2, the character 'u' precedes a string and then casts the data into Unicode. However, in the case of Python 3, Unicode is the default. However, if you wish to have backwards compatibility, then it is critical that you use the 'u' character before a string for portability of the code.

So then, should I learn Python 2.7 or 3.5? Well, the truth is as a beginner you have to think about the decline in support of version 2, and the added advantages of the upgrade. This means that it is better to use the latest version. However, say you are working on a project that requires version 2 capabilities, in such a case, it may be compelling to learn the syntax and function differences between the two versions.

The truth is, version 3 is better for you considering the fact that its support will go way into the future and this means that it will be extensively used. Trust me, it is quite difficult to go back to start learning the subtle differences in the two versions if you at some point you need to use python 2.7. With great community support, your work will be much simplified.

Installing Python on Windows

Step 1: Download Installation Files

The first thing that you have to do if you are using windows is simply open the browser window at Python.org. Then navigate to the Download page and you will see the following and then select Python for Windows as shown by the arrow;

Underneath the heading Python Releases for Windows, select the latest version release (In this case, the latest one is Python 3.7.3) as shown below;

Scroll to the bottom and then depending on whether your computer is 64-bit or 32-bit, select the option that best suits your OS.

Stable Releases

- Python 3.7.3 - March 25, 2019

  Note that Python 3.7.3 *cannot* be used on Windows XP or earlier.

  - Download Windows help file
  - Download Windows x86-64 embeddable zip file
  - Download Windows x86-64 executable installer
  - Download Windows x86-64 web-based installer
  - Download Windows x86 embeddable zip file
  - Download Windows x86 executable installer
  - Download Windows x86 web-based installer

So, here is the difference between a 64-bit and a 32-bit installer;

If your computer system has a processor that is 32-bit in capacity, then it is important that you download the 32-bit installer. If it is a 64-bit processor, either installer can actually work on your OS. This is because the 32-bit will generally use less memory while 64-bit performs much more complex and intensive computations which makes it better for applications of large projects.

However, if you are not sure which version is suitable for your OS, simply select the 64-bit version. Just remember that if you get the choice wrong and prefer switching to another version, all you have to do is uninstall Python and then reinstall by following the whole process right from downloading another installer all the way to installation.

Step 2: Preparing Installation

Once you have already downloaded a suitable Python installer fit for your Operating System, the next thing is for you to run it. Simply click on the downloaded file. A dialogue box will appear, and you need to check all the boxes at the bottom of the page to ensure that the interpreter is placed in the right execution path. Then click on the Install button. That is all there is to it.

Step 3: Complete and verify the python installation

The installation process will only take a couple of minutes and once it is completely installed, press on the Finish button on the dialogue box that will appear. By the end of this process, you will have your selected Python version 3.7.3 installed on your computer.

To verify the Python installation, simply check whether you have it. Open the terminal window on your computer and type in;

```
$ python --version
Python 3.7.3
```

If you get the above output, then the installation process was successful.

Installing Python on Mac

Step 1: Install Xcode

One thing that you have to note is that to install Python 3 on macOS, you will need package manager Homebrew to do that. However, homebrew depends on Xcode package and hence the need to run the command first to install it;

It is important to also bear in mind that Xcode is a large program and this means that it might take a long time to install subject to the strength of the internet connection. Therefore, ensure that you click through all the confirmation commands during installation.

Step 2: Install Homebrew

In spite of the fact that Python 2 is usually installed as the default python language on Apple computers, the truth is that you will need to install Python 3 latest version; in this case Python 3.7.3. Just like we have already mentioned above, the first thing that you need to do is to confirm what python version you have installed in your system;

```
$ python --version

Python 3.7.3
```

Alternatively, if you want to check whether you have python version 3 already installed in your system, simply type the following command

```
Python3 --version
```

Once you have verified that you have or do not have the latest version which at this point in 2019 is 3.7.3, then the next step would be to start the process of installing it.

First, you have to install Homebrew;

```
/usr/bin/ruby -e "$(curl -fsSL
https://raw.githubusercontent.com/Homebrew/install/master/install)"
```

Alternatively, you can simply get the Homebrew command above from the Homebrew website. The best thing about copying it directly from the website and pasting it on your command terminal is that you avoid making mistakes considering the fact that it is a long command.

Then confirm that Homebrew has been correctly installed. Simply run the command;

> *$ brew doctor*
> *Your system is ready to brew.*

Step 3: Install Python 3

In order for you to install the latest version of python3, simply run the following command;

> *$ brew install python3*
> *#then confirm the version that was installed*
> *$ python3 –version*
> *Python 3.7.3*

If you would like to open Python 3 shell from the command line, simply type in python3 and this is what you will get;

```
$ python3
Python 3.7.0 (default, Jun 29 2018, 20:13:13)
[Clang 9.1.0 (clang-902.0.39.2)] on darwin
Type "help", "copyright", "credits" or "license" for more information.
>>>
```

To exit, simply key in the command *exit()* and hit the return button or simply press *Ctrl -D* simultaneously. Additionally, note that you can still run python shell with version 2 by just type the command python and you get the following output;

```
$ python
Python 2.7.15 (default, Jun 17 2018, 12:46:58)
[GCC 4.2.1 Compatible Apple LLVM 9.1.0 (clang-902.0.39.2)] on darwin
Type "help", "copyright", "credits" or "license" for more information.
>>>
```

Python Virtual Environment

For every Python project you are working on, the most important thing that you should never forget is always to use a virtual environment. Using a virtual environment ensures that you create an isolated space that you can run different versions of Python whether 2 or 3 for various projects depending on your needs. As we already discussed in the previous chapter, to do this, you can simply use the pyenv application to achieve that.

It is also best practice to ensure that you have all your virtual environments in one place for all python projects. For instance; *.virtualenvs/* in your home directory and to create it simply type the command;

```
$ mkdir ~/.virtualenvs
#then create a new virtual environment and call it myenv
$ python3 -m pyenv ~/.virtualenvs/myenv
```

Considering the fact that we typed in python3 in the above command, each time we call python, it will automatically know that we want python version 3 and not version 2. So, for us to activate the virtual environment for use, we simply run the following command;

```
$ source ~/.virtualenvs/myvenv/bin/activate
(myvenv) $
```

Also, it is critical for us to note that while the environment is still active, its name will appear on the parenthesis. Additionally, all the software packages that we will install now will be available in the virtual environment. If you want to see all the installed software within your active virtual environment, you can simply use the command *pip freeze*. Alternatively, if you wish to stop using the virtual environment, you can completely close the terminal you are working on or enter the command deactivate;

```
(myvenv) $ deactivate
$
```

Linux System

Step 1: Check Python version and update package manager

The first thing that you should do if you are using Linux system is to check whether you already have python installed in your computer and what version it is by simply using the command;

```
$ python --version
Or
$ python3 -version
```

One thing that you have to note is that if your Linux system came with Python already installed, it might be better if you install the python developer package. This goes a long way in ensuring that you get access to all available headers and libraries that are required for compiling extensions. It also plays a very significant role in ensuring that you can install the AWS CLI.

Step 2: Installing Python 3 on Linux Mint and Ubuntu

As mentioned in the previous sections, with a Linux system, you can use various package managers to install developer package; python-dev. On Debian derivatives like Ubuntu, you simply use apt, yum or zypper to do installations.

```
$ sudo apt -get install python3
$ sudo yum install python3
$ sudo zypper install python3
```

Step 3: Installing Python 3 IDLE

Well, ever heard of Python 3 IDLE? Well, this is a graphical program that is used in writing and testing Python 3 programs. The good thing with this program is that it has a graphical user interface that makes it user-friendly. To write the python code, it is always recommended that you start doing it using python 3 IDLE. The other advantage of using this program is that it is lightweight and has an impressive syntax that highlights its abilities.

To install python 3 IDLE for the latest version of python, simply run the following command;

```
$ sudo apt -get install idle-python 3.7.3
# Press y and then the <Enter> button to start installation
```

Setting Up Environment Variables

If you are using Windows, then you are in luck because it allows permanent configuration of environment variables both at the user level and the system level. You can also perform configurations temporarily in a command prompt.

If you want to temporarily set the environment variables, the first thing that you have to do is initiate the command prompt window and the use it to set commands.

```
C:\>set PATH=C:\Program Files\Python 3.7.3; %PATH%

C:\>set PYTHONPATH-%PYTHONPATH%;C:\My_python_lib
```

One thing that you have to note is that these changes apply to other commands executed in the same console. They will also be inherited by all other applications started from that very console. When you include the name of the variable within the percentage signs, they will expand to the current value. This goes a long way in adding the new value either at the beginning or the end.

When you modify the PATH by simply adding the directory that contains python.exe to the beginning, you simply ensure that the correct python version is launched. However, if you want to make permanent modifications to the default environment variables, simply click the start button and then search for 'edit environment variables'. For you to make changes to the system variables, you will have to have Administrators rights to the machine.

Windows will ensure that the User variables are concatenated after the system variables, something that is quite unexpected when the PATH id being modified.

The variable PYTHONPATH is present in both version 2 and 3 of python. Therefore, it is important that you do not permanently configure this variable unless it includes only the code compatible with all your installed versions.

Setting up PATH in Windows

I trust that if you are using Windows OS, then the guide on installation above has helped to install it on your computer. However, one thing that we may not have mentioned above is that when you use the default installation option, the path to the executable code is not added automatically to the path variable on Windows.

The main role of the path variable is to list the directories that will be searched for executables once a command is typed in the command prompt. When you add the path to the executable python version, you simply gain access to python.exe by just typing the keyword python without necessarily having to specify the path to the program.

So, what really happens if you enter the python command in the command prompt and the path variable does not have the executables? Well this is what happens;

```
C:\>python
'python' is not recognized as either an external or internal operable program or batch file
```

The output above simply tells us that the executable command was not found. Therefore, in order to run the command python.exe, it is critical that you specify the path to where it is located;

```
C:\>C\Python3.7\python --version
Python 3.7.3
```

Therefore, to add the executable command python.exe to the path variable, the first thing is to start the Run box and then enter sysdm.cpl as shown by the image below;

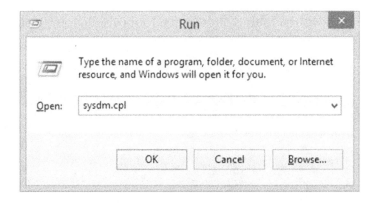

This will simply open the system properties window. Move your cursor to the Advanced tab and from the drop-down list, select Environment Variables.

From the system variable window, try to locate the path variable and then click on Edit as shown below;

Once you have clicked on the Edit tab, then move your cursor to the end of the Variable value line and then add the correct path where your executable python.exe file is located and then add a semicolon after the path. In the below example, we have added; C:\python34

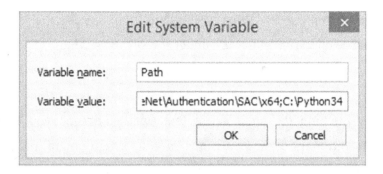

Then close all the windows and then run the executable file python.exe without now specifying the path. What is your output? If you have done this correctly, then you should get the following output

C:\>python –version
Python 3.7.3

If you are still getting a message that 'python' is not recognized…, then evidently, there is something wrong in the path variable you have given. In this case, you will need to open all the command prompt windows so that you can make proper changes to the Path Variable for the command executable file to run successfully.

Setting PATH in Mac and Linux

Now, just to recap again what we have already mentioned in previous sections, when you are working with Python, the reason why you set an environmental variable referred to as "PYTHONPATH" is so that it automatically loads the python module each time you call python. This goes a long way in helping you save as much time as possible while also eliminating the need for you to type in the whole path to the python module each time you want to use it.

If you are using macOS like me, or Unix and Linux, the unique thing with this is that you are adding the 'PYTHONPATH' variable to a shell script unlike in Windows where you are adding it to the Environmental variables screen under the system settings.

Step 1

Start by opening the shell script that runs each time you open the terminal in a text editor. In a Linux or Unix environment, the script is often referred to as bash-profile or bashrc. In the macOS environment, the file is referred to as ".profile"

Step 2

In your terminal, type the following command;

```
PYTHONPATH = "$ {PYTHONPATH} :/path/where/python/package/is/located/

export PYTHONPATH
```

For a typical Unix system or Linux OS, the path is something like; "/usr/lib/python 3.7.3/site-packages/"

On the other hand, the macOS looks like this;

```
"Library/Frameworks/Python.framework/Versions/3.7.3/lib/python3.7.3/site-packages"
```

Step 3

Once you have done that, then you just save the file. When you start a new shell, the changes that you have made get affected.

Installing PIP

Just like any other serious programming language, python offers support to a wide range of third-party libraries as well as frameworks one can install in order to avoid having to reinvent the wheel every time you have a new project. The good news is that you can find everything you need on a central repository referred to as python package index (PyPI).

However, one frustrating and time-consuming thing about this is installing and managing all these packages by hand. With the advent of such special tools as PIP for python, everything is fast and effortless.

So, what really is PIP for Python?

Well, PIP is a recursive acronym that simply stands for PIP installs Packages. Others refer to it as Preferred Installer Program. This is a command line utility that plays a central role in installation, reinstallation and uninstalling PyPI packages. It is quite straightforward because you just use a single command called pip.

The other question important question you might be asking is whether PIP is installed with Python. Well, if you are using version 2.7.9 and beyond or version 3.4 and beyond, then PIP comes along as a default program when you install python. However, if you are still using an older version (which you should upgrade!), the installation steps below will guide you on the right way to do it.

In the meantime, it is critical that you use a virtual environment when running Python which you create using pyenv we discussed in the sections above. This way, PIP will be accessible to your environment irrespective of what version you are using.

Again, just check that you have the correct version of python installed on your system;

```
python --version
```

If you have a version that falls within the categories I highlighted above, then you are good to go. If you get an error message stating that 'python' is not recognized or defined, then go back and install Python the right way as we have already discussed in previous sections.

Installing PIP on Windows

If you have windows 7,8 or 1o, the following instructions should get you a functional PIP.

Start by downloading the get-pip.py installer script from the PIP website. Right click on the link to the script and select from the list of options Save As.... Then save it to a safe location of your choice like Desktop, Downloads among others.

Then open the command prompt and navigate to locate the get-pip.py executable file from where you saved it. Run the command;

C: \>python get-pip.py #to install PIP to your system.

Installing PIP on macOS

Like we have already mentioned earlier, the Mac system often comes already installed with Python and PIP. However, in most cases the already installed Python is outdated/obsolete and is not the best kind to perform serious computational projects. Therefore, we highly recommend again that you ensure you are proceeding with the latest version of Python and PIP so that when we get started with real tasks in this tutorial, you will be ready to go!

Alternatively, if you desire to use the native system Python installation but then you do not have PIP, simply install PIP using the following command;

sudo easy_install pip

However, if you choose to install the latest version of python, simply use the Homebrew command we have discussed in previous sections just using the command;

brew install python

This will install the very recent version of python along with PIP. However, there are instances when the installation is a success but then PIP is not available. If that happens to you, simply re-link Python using the following terminal command;

brew unlink python && brew link python

Installing PIP on Linux

Just like we have already mentioned above, Python may already come installed on your Linux OS and this simply means that you can easily install PIP using your package manager. This is the best method to use since already installed python often does not work well with the script get-pip.py as it does with macOS and Windows.

Use the following command to do your installation depending on the python version and the package manager you are available to you;

```
sudo apt-get install python-pip #Python 2.x
sudo apt-get install python3-pip #Python 3.x
sudo yum upgrade python-setuptools # Python 2.x
sudo yum install python-pip python-wheel
sudo yum install python3 python3-wheel # Python 3.x
sudo zypper install python-pip python-setuptools python-wheel # Python 2.x
sudo zypper install python3-pip python3-setuptools python3-wheel # Python 3.x
```

Upgrading PIP for Python

One thing that is important to note is that PIP does not upgrade itself often. This means that the trick is for you to ensure that you stay on top of new python versions as much as possible because that is how you get important fixes to bugs, security holes as well as compatibility issues. That said, upgrading pip is quite simple and super-fast.

On windows you can use the command python -m pip install -U pip, while on Mac/Linux you can use the command Pip install -U pip

Managing python packages with PIP

Once you already have PIP ready, the next thing is for you to start installing packages from PyPI;

One important thing to remember is that as your packages become outdated, PIP automatically removes them when you decide to upgrade to a newer version of the same.

Chapter Five

Running Python on your device

L et's take a look at how you can run your python code on a Windows PC

First of all, you need to understand that python does not come pre-installed on your Windows PC. So you need first to install it. Wondering where to get the Python installer? Don't worry; we got you. The saddest part is that people who are ready and willing to learn Python struggle in silence.

This happened to many, and it is always wise to seek advice from reliable experts in the field. Note, however, that once you follow the instructions provided below for sure your programming life will change. As history dictates, Python is a self-inspired programming language.

The creator had a vision in designing this program. Guido Van Rossum Python program will forever be a programming language that will go down the history books of coding.

In the installation chapter, you will get to know where and how to install the Python program to your device.

Installing Python on Windows

After accessing the installation link, you will land on the Python's download page. Just click on the Python download button, and a pop up will appear showing you the installer's size. The installer is mainly about 29MB, and with good internet speed, you can get the download in a couple of minutes.

Once you have the Python installer in your computer, move it either to a safe hard drive partition for future use. Once you are done, double-click the installer so that installation can be initiated.

A pop up will appear asking you to run it. Click Run and wait patiently for the next stage. A page will appear with options to Install Now, Customize installation. A checkbox asking if you would like to install it for all the users will appear.

It is recommended to click on the install for all users checkbox and then clicks on the Install Now button. Due to the inbuilt security features inbuilt in the Windows OS, User account control pops up will manifest asking for permission to write the installer to your hard drive, click yes.

On clicking this, the installation process should start. Wait until the setup process is complete then close the installer. Verify installation afterward.

Verifying Python Installation

The most important thing is to get the file directory where Python has been installed. To make things simple, it is important that you understand that a directory is a folder in the computer where files of the same caliber have been installed.

Verification is important so you can make sure that you have the software — counter check to make sure that there are no present errors.

Since you now know Python's directory, navigate to it
C:\Users\{USER}\AppData\Local\Programs\Python\Python37-32

After you have found it. Look for a file by the name python.exe, double-click it, and then a window will appear.

Configure your Python installation

To run Python smoothly without any issues, it is recommended to tweak environment settings on windows. This keeps you away from all the inconveniences as a beginner that may make your life hard while learning Python.

This gives Python the environment it requires to execute commands and run .py scripts accordingly. Without handling this configuration, it may seem tricky because the directories can be hard to find and as said before programmers tend to have neat computers.

Set the environmental variables

It may sound like a daunting task. However, contrary to that, it is quite easy to learn. It only requires your will to learn as a newbie - you have to remain focused throughout. Normally, Windows environment variables are easy to find and adjust. Just click On This PC in Windows 10 or click My Computer in previous versions.

Right click on the blank space. Click on Properties. On the top left, you'll see Advanced System Settings. Upon clicking, a folder will pop with the environment variable button on the bottom click on it. You will need administrator rights to achieve non-restricted access.

On the other hand, there is a second way of changing the environmental variables permanently. This is by using the msconfig by adding set PYTHONPATH=%PYTHONPATH%; C:\My_python_lib to the autoexec.bat. Even though this seems like a hassle, it will get your variable changed.

Other than those two methods, you can quickly switch to your command prompt and type echo %PATH%.

Running Python on Windows

This is like starting an engine of a project car that you have been working on for five years. Think of all the fun part of installing all the requirements then executing .py scripts that make you hungry for more knowledge and code in Android.

Honestly, running a Python program on windows without the Python installer makes no sense. What is the point of coding a Python script and then finding out later on that your computer cannot execute the script? For sure, it's going to be pointless.

That is why you have the above guide with easy steps for installing and configuring Python into your computer.

Run Python Using Command Prompt in Windows

To run your Python script using the Command prompt, you are required to pass the path of the script as an argument to the Python interpreter. As earlier stated, you have to know the directory of the Python interpreter to copy the full path of the Python interpreter. Here is an example

python.exe C: \Users\User2\Desktop\my_python_script.py.

As a beginner, you should know that Windows has 2 Python executables, which are python.exe and pythonw.exe. It is mostly used in GUI programs where you want to view the graphical user interface of the program, not the terminals.

Run Python Script as a File

Most programmers I know often tend to create standalone scripts that are independent to live environments. It is often saved as .py which notifies the operating system that it is a Python program. Since the operating system is aware that it is a Python file, the interpreter is invoked and interprets and reads the file.

Have you ever heard of programmers saying that Windows-based Python scripts are very different from Linux based ones? It is true.

Running Python on a Mac

If your PC operates using the Mac software, you can still download the Python programmer. The only thing you should worry about is if you are doing it right. Running Python on Mac requires you to have lots of software, but since you are reading this, let us see if it is achievable.

Below is a step by step guideline on how to perfectly install Python on your Mac operating system and ensure that all its entities are working accordingly. There is a set of tools that Mac PCs require to create the environment for it to execute Python programs. Trust me; you won't miss out in any of the necessary tools to enable you to get what you have been missing.

Installing Python on a Mac

Before you get another cup of coffee, take your time, and install Xcode. Xcode is the official Apple's integrated development environment. You can easily get it at the App Store. Even though it is a big file, it works your time and the whole download process.

It is surely a long process, and I can assure you that you might find a nap good to kill time. Once you have the Xcode installed on your Mac, you will still be required to install the Apple command line tools. Don't stress yourself; they are quite easy to find.

Just run the Xcode program then click on preferences, go to downloads tab then look for command line tools and install it. It is as easy as taking a walk in the park.

Initiate the Terminal

I bet if you are interested in Python, you have once or twice opened the terminal and got a hint of what was going on. If you have never opened terminal, it is a nice start to get familiar with it. As a programmer, you need to have a neat computer. I store all my code in a folder by the name projects.

In a terminal, it is a rule always to start your command line instructions. For instance, if you type $ cd, it means change directory. If you don't indicate on the code where you want your command to go, it goes to the home directory by default.

Another example is when you type the $mkdir code; it means make directory.

Install Python

Luckily, Python comes installed in macOS. Here, downloading and installing isn't necessary. You can input the Python version into the terminal. If the outcome is an error message, too bad for you, you'll have to install Python manually. But if it displays Python 2.7.3, this means you are okay to proceed to the next step.

If you feel the need of getting the latest version of Python, you are required to start Homebrew. This is a requirement followed by the command you want to use. Let's say you need to install Python; then the code is $ brew install python. If you are willing to learn, this will not present itself as a challenge because you need your Mac to execute your Python programs.

Install GIT

GIT keeps track of all your previous codes which you can view in different devices simultaneously. It helps in merging your code with all the other programmers' codes and leads you to collaborate.

You will be able to meet your online peers who share the same vision as you and get to do more work at a minimal time. You are likely to land jobs that will aid you in building your portfolio. It has a huge community that is supportive of every time.

Run a Python Script on a Mac or Linux

Normally, in a Mac or Linux OS, you have the freedom to put a shebang line as the first line of the program. Which very fast finds the location of the Python interpreter on the Mac.

Example: *#!/path/to/interpreter*

The regularly used shebang line is example #!/usr/bin/env python

To make your script executable, you will have to use the command

```
chmod +x my_python_script.py
```

As compared to windows, Python interpreter is in the $PATH environmental variable.

Here is how you can invoke the interpreter and run a Python program manually: Python firstprogram.py

Chapter Six

How to organize the Python Code

Python Keywords

The following words (also called keywords) are the base of the Python language. You cannot use these words to name an identifier or a variable in your program since they are considered the core words of the language. They cannot be misspelled and must be written in the same way for the interpreter to understand what you want the system to do. Some of the words include; False, None, assert, True, as, break, continue, def, import, in, is, and, class, del, for, from, global, raise, return, else, if, not, or, pass, except, try, while, with, finally, if, lambda, nonlocal, and yield among others.

Naming Identifiers

By using identifiers in Python, you will be providing a name to the class, variable, function, module, or any other object that is being used in Python. Identifiers will always start with a letter that is either uppercase or lowercase. Identifiers can also start with underscores that are followed by a zero, letters, another underscore, or numbers.

You cannot use punctuation when you are creating identifiers. It is vital to remember that, when you are using Python, identifiers need to be case sensitive. This means you need to pay special attention to what you are entering. Simple words like *bell* and *Bell* are two different identifiers even though they are the same word. They are different because of how they are written; one is capitalized, and the other is not.

While you are working with identifiers, there are a few things that you need to keep in mind:

1. Private identifiers start with an underscore and are different than strongly private identifiers.

2. Any identifier that has two underscores at the end is considered a special name identifier.

3. Strongly private identifiers start with two underscores.

4. Whenever an uppercase letter is at the beginning of the class name, the identifier that follows is lowercase.

Rules for Writing Identifiers

Identifiers have rules that you need to follow when writing them. Otherwise, Python is not going to accept the identifier. The rules are simple, but must be applied to each identifier that is entered into Python:

1. You are not allowed to use a number as the first character in the identifier.

Example: 5cat

2. Identifiers are a sequence of both numbers and characters.

Example: made4you

3. Capitalization is extremely significant because Python is a case-sensitive program.

Example: Cup vs. cup

4. You should not use keywords in the identifier's name.

Example: trynotassetpass

5. There cannot be any other special character in your identifier other than an underscore.

Example: *not#me1

Exploring Variables

Let's talk about the words that you can use and those you cannot. Every variable name must always begin with an underscore or a letter. Some variables can contain numbers, but they cannot start with one. If the interpreter comes across a set of variables that begin with a number instead of quotation marks or a letter, it will only consider that variable as a number. You should never use anything other than an underscore, number, or letter to identify a variable in your code. You must also remember that Python is a case-sensitive language; therefore, false and False are two different entities. The same can be said for vvariable, Vvariable, and VVariable. As a beginner, you must make a note of all the variables you use in your code. This will also help you find something easier in your code.

Every variable is created in two stages; the first stage is used to initialize the variable, and the second is used to assign a value to that variable. In the first step, you must create a variable and name it appropriately to stick a label on it, and in the second step, you must put a value in the variable. These steps are performed using a single command in Python that utilizes the equal-to sign. When you must assign a value, you should write the following code:

```
Variable = value
```

Every section of the code that performs some function, like an assignment, is called a statement. The part of the code that can be evaluated to obtain value is called an expression. Let us take a look at the following example:

```
Length = 14
Breadth = 10
Height = 10
Area_Triangle = Length * Breadth * Height
```

Any variable can be assigned a value, or an expression, like the assignment made to Area_Triangle in the example above.

Every statement must be written in a separate line. If you write the statements down the same way you would write down a shopping list, you are doing it the right way. Every recipe begins in the same way with a list of ingredients and the proportions along with the equipment that you need to use to complete your dish. The same happens when you write a Python code; you first define the variables you want to use and then create functions and methods to use on those variables.

Recognizing Different Types of Variables

The interpreter in Python recognizes different types of variables - sequences or lists, numbers, words or string literals, booleans, and mappings. These variables are often used in Python programs. A variable None has a type of its own called NoneType. Before we look at how words and numbers can be used in Python, we must first look at the dynamic typing features.

Working with Variables in this Language

When you assign a value to a variable, the interpreter will decide the type of value the variable is, which is called "dynamic typing." Unlike other languages, Python does not require the user to declare the types of variables being utilized in the program. This can be considered both a blessing and a curse. The advantage is that you do not have to worry about the variable type when you write the code, and you only need to worry about the way the variable behaves.

Dynamic typing in Python makes it easier for the interpreter to handle user input that's unpredictable. The interpreter for Python accepts different forms of user input to which it assigns a dynamic type. This means that a single statement can be used to deal with numbers, words, or other data types, and the user does not always have to know what data type the variable must be. Not needing to declare variables before you use them makes it tempting to introduce variables at random places in your scripts. You must remember that Python won't complain unless you try to use a variable before you have assigned it a value, but it's really easy to lose track of what variables you are using and where you set up their values in the script.

Two really sensible practices will help keep you sane when you start to create large numbers of different variables. One is to set up a bunch of default values at the start of each section if you're sure of where you will need to use them. It is always a good idea to group all the variables. The other is to keep track of the expected types and values of your variables, keeping a data table in your design document for each program that you're writing.

The API in Python will need to keep track of the variable type for a few reasons. The machine will need to set some memory aside to store this information. The different data types in Python take up different volumes of space. The second reason is that keeping track of types helps to avoid and troubleshoot errors. Once Python has decided what type a variable is, it will flag up a TypeError if you try to perform an inappropriate operation on that data. Although this might at first seem to be an unnecessary irritation, you'll discover that this can be an incredibly useful feature of the language, as the following command-line example shows:

```
>>> b = 3
>>> c = 'word'
>>> trace = False
>>>
b + c
Traceback (most recent call last):
File "", line 1, in <module>
TypeError: unsupported operand type(s) for +: 'int' and 'str'
>>> c - trace
Traceback (most recent call last):
File "", line 1, in <module>
TypeError: unsupported operand type(s) for -: 'str' and 'bool'
```

The program above attempts to operate data types that are incompatible. You're not allowed to add a number to a word or take a yes/no answer away from it. It is necessary to convert the data to a compatible type before trying to process it. You can add words together or take numbers away from each other just like you can in real life, but you can't do arithmetic on a line of text. Python will alert you if there is some error in your logic using tracebacks. In this case, it gives you the TypeError. This error will let you know that you must rewrite the code to ensure that you let the compiler know what type of information you should put in. This information is dependent on the output that you want to obtain.

The purpose of data types is to allow you to represent information that exists in the real world (the world that exists outside your computer) as opposed to the virtual world inside. (We can have the existential conversation about what is real and what is not some other time.) The previous example uses variables of type int (whole numbers) and types str (text). It will quickly become apparent that these basic data types can only represent the simplest units of information; you may need to use quite a complicated set of words, numbers, and relationships to describe even the simplest real-world entity in virtual-world terms.

Python provides a variety of ways to combine these simple data types to create more complex data types, which we'll come to later in the book. First, you need to know about the fundamental building blocks that are used to define your data and the basic set of actions you can use to manipulate the different types of values.

The None Variable

A predefined variable called None is a special value in Python. It has a type of its own and is useful when you need to create a variable without defining or specifying a value to it. When you assign values such as "and 0, the interpreter will define the variable as the str or int variable.

A variable can be assigned the value None using the statement above. The next few examples will use real-world information that will be modeled into a virtual form using some fantasy characters. This example uses some statistics to represent a few attributes of the characters to provide data for the combat system. You can use this example to automate your database and your accounts. So, let's take a look at some of the characters in the example.

In the program, hello_world.py, you saw how you could get a basic output using the print () function. This function can be used to print out the value of the variable and a literal string of characters. Often, each print statement must start on a new line, but several values can be printed on a single line by using a comma to separate them; print () can then be used to concatenate all the variables into a single line only separated by spaces.

```
>>> Race = "Goblin"
>>> Gender = "Female"
>>> print (Gender, Race)
Female Goblin
```

Different segments of information can be combined into a single line using multiple methods. Some of these methods are more efficient when compared to others. Adjacent strings that are not separated will be concatenated automatically, but this is not a function that works for most variables.

```
>>> print ("Male" "Elf")
```

The expression above will give you the following output: "MaleElf."

However, when you enter the following code,

```
>>> print ("Male" Race)
```

You will receive the following error:

```
File "<stdin>", line 1
print ("Male" Race)
     ^
SyntaxError: invalid syntax
```

This approach cannot be used since you can't write a string function as a variable and a string together since this is just a way of writing a single line string.

It is straightforward to assign any number to variables.

```
Muscle = 8
Brains = 13
```

If any variable begins with a number, the interpreter will view that variable as a number, even if there are some other characters used in that variable. It is for this reason that you should never name a variable starting with a number. There are a few points that you will need to keep in mind before you work with numbers.

Writing Comments in YourCode

Not everything inside of a command prompt is going to be executed by the program. What is not executed are the comments that are inserted by the developer. The comments help other developers understand what is going on in the program or allow them to pick up the code where the previous developer left off. These comments can also indicate whenever the code has been changed if the code has to be changed again later.

Comments are easy to spot in the Python code because they are offset by a hashtag, and they are always located on a command line after the code has been entered.

> *Example:*
> *#!/ usr/bin/Python*
> *#the comment will go here*
> *Print "Thesearenotmymonkeys" #you can put another comment in right here!*

The output will be: These are not my monkeys

So, even though the comment is on the same line as the coding, the program knows not to print the comment because it is offset by a special character.

Comments are also able to expand across multiple lines, so you get a better understanding of what is going on within the code. It does not matter where in the code your comment goes because the interpreter is going to skip over it while executing the code.

Example:

> *#first comment*
> *#comment number two*
> *#your comments can say anything that you want them to say*
> *#Hello, I hope you are learning a lot from this book!*

Working with Operators

Math is part of our daily lives even if we do not realize it. The programs that we use each day are going to incorporate math that we do not see because it is automatically programmed to do the math in the code that the developer wrote. Doing simple math is easy for everyone, but when it is not simple, that is when most people prefer to have some help from other tools. This is where Python comes in.

It is easy to place your equation into a program and read off the result, which is exactly what Python does for you! However, your result is dependent on you placing the correct equation into the program. If you are not placing the proper equation into the program, then you will get the wrong answer. However, it does not matter if you are working with simple math or complex equations: Python can do it all!

Here are some of the most common operators that you will use while you are working with Python:

1. Modulo (%)
2. Addition (+)
3. Floor division (//)
4. Square root (math.sqrt)
5. Negation (-x)
6. Subtraction (-)
7. Division (/)
8. Exponent (a**n)
9. Absolute value (abs())
10. Multiplication (*)

Keep in mind that, while using the square root function, you will be required to load the math module for that particular operation. While doing this, you will be entering a code that is listed at the top of the file being used.

A bad thing about math is that, with Python, there are some limitations that you will run into with floating point numbers, as well as the rounding of these numbers. A lot of users experience error messages or even unexpected results. For example, while dividing a floating-point number (6.0 / 2.0), you will receive the correct answer. However, while doing floor division, you will get an output of a number that does not make sense for the equation that was entered.

Floor division was first introduced in the 2x version of Python as a solution for working with integers and longs. However, the true division has to be used while working with complex or float numbers because the results can be unexpected. As you move on and look at Python 3.x, the true division was created to make sure that it can be used on any number that is entered into the program. However, users still experience issues.

The issues can be solved by inserting a set of parentheses around the division sign so that whenever the program rounds, you will receive the proper answer.

Another thing that you should keep in mind is that math will always use the PEMDAS system. You most likely learned this in elementary school and thought that you'd never use it again. Sorry about this, but here it is again, and it will be used by the Python program while it executes the equations entered into its code.

Here is a little refresher of what the acronym PEMDAS stands for:

P - <u>P</u>arentheses

E - <u>E</u>xponents

M - <u>M</u>ultiplication

D - <u>D</u>ivision

A - <u>A</u>ddition

S - <u>S</u>ubtraction

Example:

$8 + (32 - 2) * 2 / 4 - 2 = ?$

If you follow the PEMDAS rules, the first step will be the <u>P</u>arentheses.

$8 + (32 - 2) * 2 / 4 - 2 \rightarrow 8 + (30) * 2 / 4 - 2$

Next is the <u>E</u>xponent. If you examine the equation, you will notice that there are no exponents. Therefore, you can move on to the next step, which is <u>M</u>ultiplication.

$8 + (30) * 2 / 4 - 2 \rightarrow 8 + 60 / 4 - 2$

Next will be <u>D</u>ivision.

$8 + 60 / 4 - 2 \rightarrow 8 + 15 - 2$

Then, <u>A</u>ddition.

$8 + 15 - 2 \rightarrow 23 - 2$

And finally, <u>S</u>ubtraction.

$23 - 2 \rightarrow 21$

As you can see, there are a lot of steps, but this is what Python does behind the scenes to provide you with the proper answer to your mathematical equation.

Comparison and Relational Operators

Comparison operators examine the values that fall on each side and determine what the relationship is between them. You may also know these as relational operators.

The operators are:

1. <=: The value that is found on the left side is less than or equal to the value that is found on the right side. If this is correct, then the condition is marked as true.

   Example: 2 <= 4

2. ==: The values are equal. If this is correct, then the value is true.

   Example: 6 == 6

3. >=: The value that is found on the left side is equal to or greater than the value that is found on the right. If this is correct, then the condition is found to be true.

   Example: 6 >= 2

4. !=: The values are not equal, and if they are not, then the condition is true.

   Example: 1 != 4

5. <: The value on the left is less than the value on the right.

   Example: 4 < 9

6. >: The value on the left is greater than the value on the right.

   Example: 9 >3

Assignment Operators

Assignment operators explain where the value is assigned after the function is complete.

1. //=: This is used with floor division. The operator is assigned to the value that is located on the left.

   Example: 4 //= 2 equals 4 =// 2

2. =: The value on the right is always assigned to the value found on the left.

   Example: 4 = 2 + 2

3. **=: The exponent and this go before the exponent first, and then everything is assigned to the left side.

   Example: 4 **= 2 equals 4 = 4 ** 2

4. +=: "Add" and the right operator are added together before being assigned to the left side.

   Example: 4 += 2 equals 4 = 4 + 2

5. %=: Modulus and the modulus are done before it is all moved to the left side.

   Example: 4 %= 2 equals 4 = 4 % 2

6. -=: Subtract and subtraction are done before moving it to the left.

   Example: 4 -= 2 equals 4 = 4 - 2

7. /=: Divide and division are done before everything is moved to the left.

Example: 4 /= 2 equals 4 = 4 / 2

8. *=: Multiple and multiplication are placed on the result before it is moved over to the left.

Example: 4 *= 2 equals 4 = 4 * 2

The Functions in Python

Python has things that are known as user-defined functions. These functions are declarations that are made, and they always start with the def keyword, followed by the function's name.

Many functions are arguments because they are inputted at the beginning and the closing of parentheses. Once the name of the function has been inputted, it is followed by a colon.

After the function has been defined, the arguments that are set for that block of code, which is located on the next line, are executed, followed by any line that is indented.

Syntax:

```
Def function_name (argument 1, argument 2, ...) :
Statement_ 1
Statement _ 2
```

Calling a Function

Whenever a function is called on by Python, you are following a process that is similar to what you may have seen in other programming languages. You need to use the name of the function, as well as a set of parentheses, and then, the parameters will follow.

Syntax:

> *Function_name (arg 1, arg 2)*

Example:

> *Def avg_amount (n, o):*
> *Print ("the average of "n" and "o" is, (n + o) / 3")*
> *Average_amount (5, 9)*

The result is what your average is for the numbers of five and nine.

Sounds confusing, right? Let's break it down further so that you can understand it a little better.

- Lines 1 + 2: These hold the definition for your function.

- Line 1: Here is where you lay out your parameters.

- Line 2: This is where you print the value for your parameters, as well as what it is that you defined in the function.

- Line 3: This is where the function is called on.

There is a possibility that you will have a function that does not have an argument tied to it, and that is perfectly fine, but it will be a special case as to what Python does with it.

Syntax:

> *Def function_name():*
> *Statement_ 1*
> *Statement _ 2*

Example:

```
Def print ():
Print ("This is my house")
Print ("Here is another house")
Print ("This is my dream car")
Print ()
Result:
This is my house
Here is another house
This is my dream car.
```

Let's break down the example so that it is easier for you to understand.

- Lines 1 - 4: These hold the definition for your function.

- Line 1: There are no parameters. Therefore, this aspect is ignored.

- Lines 2 - 4: The commands are carried out and printed as they should be.

- Line 5: The function is called on here.

Using Functions to Call Other Functions

When using a function to call another function, you do the same thing that you did when you called on the function in the first place. It is one of the many advantages that you have while working with Python. The biggest difference is that you are defining the function that has already been used instead of defining the printme function.

Chapter Seven

Mastering Data Preparation with Python

Have you been thinking of ways in which you can master your data preparation with Python? Well, this is the right place! Whether you choose to use the term data preparation, cleaning, cleansing, pre-processing, or wrangling, they all refer to the same thing. These terms simply refer to pre-modeling data activities that take place in the machine learning and mining communities.

Data cleaning can be defined as the process through which one detects and corrects inaccurate records from a data set, database or tables and then replacing or deleting the dirty data. The good thing with data cleaning is that you can perform it interactively using data wrangling tools or processing them as a batch through the user of python scripts.

On the other hand, you can think of data wrangling as a manual process through which data is converted or mapped from one raw form to another form which permits for a more convenient interpretation of data using the help of semi-automated tools.

This often includes munging, visualizing, aggregating, training a model, among other potential uses. Data munging simply refers to the process by which one follows a set of steps that start with raw data extraction from a source, and then munging it using algorithms or parsing it into a well-defined structure which is finally deposited into a data sink for storage as well as use in the future.

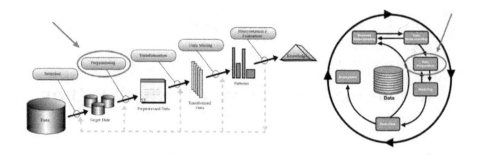

Data preparation in both the <u>KDD Process</u> (left) and the <u>CRISP-DM model</u> (right).

Here are some of the steps that will help you master how to prepare your data for analysis with python;

Step 1: Preparing for the Preparation

This data preparation step is not a preliminary step taken before the machine learning task. Instead, it is an integral component of what machine learning would typically cover. However, we will try as much as possible to separate data preparation from modeling in this book.

Data preparation is shown by the CRISP-DM model shown in the figure above. We could also think of data preparation in the form of the KDD process shown above; and more specifically, the first three steps that entail; data selection, preprocessing, and transformation. This is further broken down into a much finer granularity. However, at a macro level, the steps shown in the KDD process above can be thought of as data wrangling.

Step 2: Exploratory Data Analysis

This serves as an integral component of data preparation and analysis in a machine learning project. It is not just a good idea for you to understand the data you have before working on it. It is also a high priority if you are planning on doing something that yields good results.

The main role of exploratory data analysis is so that you can utilize summary statistics and visualization to gain a deeper understanding of data and so that you can be able to find clues about data tendency, quality as well as formulate assumptions and hypothesis of your analysis.

One thing that you have to bear in mind is that you need to know your data makeup before selecting predictive algorithms. It is also important for mapping out the remaining steps of your data preparation. One mistake that many people tend to make is throwing their datasets to an algorithm and then sitting back and hoping that they will get good results. Trust me that is not a strategy to go by.

Understand that for a python-based approach requires that you perform Pandas profiling to help you create HTML reports using Pandas DataFrames. Here, you can use the function df.describe (), which serves as a great function when performing exploratory data analysis. However, this function is a little basic if you are doing serious EDA. In that case, you can choose to use pandas_profiling to extend the pandas DataFrame along with the df.profile_report() for fast and seamless data analysis.

This is something that you can run interactively on Jupyter notebook we discussed earlier in this book using a single line code;

df.profile_report()

Step 3: Dealing with Missing Values

The next thing that you need to do when preparing your data is to check whether there are values that are missing. There are so many strategies that can help you deal with this, and none of them is universally applicable. There are those that will ask you never to use instances that have empty values while others will ask you never to use attribute's mean values in place of missing values. In other cases, some strategies ask you to use more complex approaches in which you first cluster the dataset into known numerical classes and then use intra-cluster regression to calculate what the missing values are.

The point is, you should not listen to such strategies as "only" or "never" among other inflexible assertions. The truth is, different kinds of data and analysis will suggest various forms of best practices for handling missing data. However, one thing that you need to understand is that this is something that is based on both experience and domain. In that case, we will focus mainly on basic strategies you can employ. Some of these include;

1. Drop instances with missing values

2. Drop attributes with missing values

3. Impute attribute's means, median or mode for all the missing values

4. Impute the attribute missing values using linear regression

You can also use these strategies in combination; dropping instances that have more than two values missing and then choosing to go with the mean attributes value imputations of those that remain. Truthfully, the type of model you use will affect the kind of decision you make.

For instance; decision trees may not be amenable in case of missing values. On the other hand, you can technically entertain various statistical approaches you can think of in determining what the missing value is from the dataset.

Because we are mainly focusing on the Python ecosystem, you can read deeply on how to work with missing data by referring to the Pandas user guide. Notice that there are various ways in which one can deal with missing values, and one of them is Pandas DataFrame. Consider the following basics;

```
# Drop the columns where all elements are missing values:
df.dropna(axis=1, how='all')


# Drop the columns where any of the elements are missing values
df.dropna(axis=1, how='any')


# Keep only the rows which contain two missing values maximum
df.dropna(thresh=2)


# Drop the columns where any of the elements are missing values
df.dropna(axis=1, how='any')


# Fill all missing values with the mean of the particular column
df.fillna(df.mean())


# Fill any missing value in column 'A' with the column median
df['A'].fillna(df['A'].median())


# Fill any missing value in column 'Depeche' with the column mode
df['Depeche'].fillna(df['Depeche'].mode())
```

Step 4: Dealing with Outliers

One important thing that we have to bear in mind is that there are times when including outliers in modeling is suitable, and there are instances that this is not a good idea. In other words, dealing with outliers is dependent on the situation at hand. Therefore, no one can make such assertions as to whether or not your situation falls under category A or B.

There are so many reasons why a dataset can have outliers. For instance, it may be an indicator of poor data collection or the data can be genuinely good and anomalous. These two scenarios, though different, must be approached in unique ways. In other words, 'one size fits all' approach is not applicable in this case, just as is when dealing with missing values.

One way to deal with these outliers is to try performing the transformation. This is mainly because square roots, as well as log transformations, have the ability to pull in high numbers, hence making assumptions work better, especially if the outlier is a dependent variable. On the other hand, this reduces the impact of a single point in case the outlier is an independent variable.

There are various ways in which you can deal with outliers. However, in the end, the decision as to whether to remove them or not will depend on the task you are performing. The bottom line is, the reasoning behind what action to take will be more of a concern than a technical approach.

Step 5: Dealing with Imbalanced Data

One question that I hear so many people asking is if their dataset is composed of 2 major classes with one instance having 95% and the other 5% of the components or even worse 99% and the other just 1%.

The truth is, when this is observed, the dataset is imbalanced as far as the classes are anything to go by, and this is especially problematic. So, should you toss your data to the side? Not! There are so many strategies that you can employ to deal with such a problem.

A very good explanation of why this happens and the reason why this is something you can frequently do in some domains compared to others is as follows; Data used in such cases often have less than a percent of interesting events that are quite rare. The problem is that most machine learning algorithms do not work very well with imbalanced datasets. With the help of the following techniques, you can train a classifier to specifically detect any abnormal class.

While this may not be a task aimed at preparing data, it is their features that often make it known early in the stage of data preparation. You can also assess the validity of such data, especially during this preparation stage.

These techniques include;

1. Using the right evaluation metrics

One of the most dangerous things you can do is using the wrong evaluation metrics for models that are generated using a dataset that is imbalanced. Consider the graph above. Imagine that this is how your training data looks like. In such a case, if accuracy is used as a measure of goodness, then this means that a model that classified all testing samples into class 0 will have a 99% accuracy. However, such a model will not offer us any valuable information.

In such a situation, you can apply other alternative evaluation metrics such as;

- AUC which offers the relationships between a true positive and a false positive rate
- Recall/Sensitivity which tells us how many relevant instances are selected
- MCC which gives the correlation coefficient between observed and predicted binary classifications
- F1 score that tells us the harmonic mean of recall and precision

2. Resampling the training set

You can work on getting a different dataset by either performing oversampling or under-sampling.

Under-sampling: this plays a very critical role in balancing the dataset by simply reducing the size of the most abundant class. This is especially used when the quantity of data is adequate. It works by keeping all the samples in the rare class and then selecting an equal number of samples in the most abundant class. This way, you end up with a balanced dataset that you can use for further modeling.

Over-sampling: on the other hand, oversampling refers to when the quantity of data is not sufficient. In such a case, python will try to balance the dataset by simply increasing the number of rare samples and instead of getting rid of the most abundant class, new rare samples are produced using bootstrapping values or Synthetic Minority Over-Sampling techniques (SMOTE).

One thing that you have to note is that there is no absolute advantage of one method over the other. Your choice of application of these two methods often depends on the use case as well as the dataset itself. It has also been shown that a combination of these two techniques is also very successful.

3. Using K-fold cross-validation the right way

It is important to note that when using cross-validation, you should do it the right way, especially when you use it along with oversampling in addressing an imbalance in the dataset. Always bear in mind that when an oversampling is applied, it takes rare samples and then applies them to bootstrapping to create random data based on the function of the distribution.

On the other hand, if you are performing cross-validation after doing oversampling, then what you are doing is overfitting your model to a specific artificial bootstrap outcome. This is the reason why cross-validation has to always come before oversampling the dataset. When you are resampling the data over and over again, there is a chance that you will introduce randomness into your dataset, making sure that overfitting problems do not occur.

4. Ensemble various resampled datasets

One of the easiest ways in which you can generalize a model successfully is through the use of more data. The only problem with this is that the out-of-the-box classifiers such as random forest or logistic regression will normally tend to generalize by simply getting rid of the rare class.

The best thing to do in such a case is to build n models that utilize all the samples in the rare class along with n-differing samples in the abundant class. Considering that you would want to ensemble ten models, you would then keep say 1.000 cases of the rare class and then select at least 10.000 cases of the abundant class. Then you split the 10 cases into ten chunks and use that to train ten different models.

n models with changing data samples for the abundant class

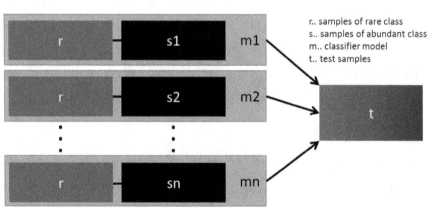

The good thing with this kind of approach is that it is simple and perfectly scalable horizontally, especially when you have a lot of data. This is mainly because all you have to do is train and run various models on different cluster nodes. The other thing is that ensemble models often generalize better, making the approach easy to handle.

5. Resample with various ratios

The approach that we have just discussed above can be further fine-tuned by simply playing around with the ratios between the abundant and rare class. This is because the best ratio often relies on the data as well as the models used. Rather than training all models with the same ratio in the ensemble, what you can do is ensemble different ratios. In other words, if you have 10 trained models, what might make lots of sense is to have a model that has a 1:1 ratio between the abundant and the rare class, and another with 1:3 ratio and another with something like 2:1 ratio; and based on the model that is used, you can influence the weight that each class gets.

n models with changing ratio between rare and abundant class

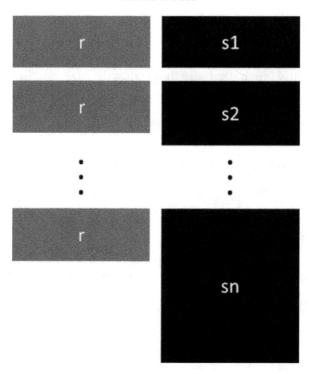

6. Clustering the abundant class

This is an elegant approach that was proposed by Sergey on Quora. Rather than depending on random samples to cover a variety of training samples, what you can do is cluster the abundant class in r groups, (r being the number of cases). Then, for each of the groups, what you keep is the medoid or the center cluster. You then train this model using the rare class and the medoids alone.

7. Designing own models

All the above methods we have discussed focus mainly on the data and then keeps the models as a fixed component. However, there is no need to resample the data when, in fact, the model is better suited for an imbalanced dataset.

A good starting point, in this case, is the use of XGBoost, especially if the classes you are dealing with are too skewed. This is mainly because it will take care internally such that the bags it will train are not imbalanced. However, the data is again resampled, only that this is something that is secretly happening.

When you design a cost function that penalizes wrong classifications of the rare class and not wrong classifications of the abundant class, what you are doing in effect is designing many models that will naturally be in favor of the rare class.

For instance, you can tweak SVM to penalize wrong classifications of the rare class using similar ratios that a class is under-represented as shown below.

Data

Cost

That said, one thing that you have to bear in mind is that the techniques we have discussed here serve as a starting point on how best to handle an imbalanced dataset. The truth is, no one approach is best suited for all problems. Therefore, it is advisable that you try as many techniques as you possibly can to assess one that works best for your case. Try as much as you can to be creative by combining various approaches.

Step 6: Data Transformations

Data transformation refers to the application of a mathematical function to every point of a dataset. In other words, each data point z_i is replaced with a transformed value y_i, such that $y_i = f(z_i)$, where f refers to a function. The reason for transformation is such that the dataset in which it is applied appears to closely satisfy the assumptions of statistical inference or rather improve the ability to interpret the data as well as graphical appearance.

One of the most important aspects of data preparation is data transformation, something that requires finesse than any other. When you have missing values manifesting in your dataset, you can easily spot them and address them using the methods we have discussed above. However, when data transformation is required, it may not be easy to identify.

Some of the most important pre-processing transformations include; binarization, standardization, and normalization. The last two are a pair of techniques that are often applied in machine learning projects. In other words, they are often used as data scaling methods. Standardization refers to the ability to scale data such that its mean is 0, and its standard deviation is 1. On the other hand, normalization refers to the ability to scale data values so that they fit into a predetermined range of say 1 and 1.

The other method that you can employ is the use of logarithmic distribution to perform the transformation of non-linear models into linear models. This can also be used when handling data that is rather skewed.

There are many other standard data transformations that you can employ regularly depending on your data as well as requirements. Once you gain more experience in data pre-processing and preparation, you will gain a deeper insight into various types of data transformations and what circumstance to apply them.

Step 7: Finishing Touches & Moving Ahead

Now that your data is already clean, what next?

The next thing you can do is feed your data right into a machine learning algorithm to build a model. In such an instance, you will first need to put your data in a more appropriate representation. In the python environment, this would be a Numpy array. In other words, that would be represented in a matrix format.

The other question that many people ask is what is it that they can do if they are not quite ready to model their data. Well, if you want just to store your data for future use, you can follow the **Quick HDF5 with Pandas**.

Chapter Eight

Data Preprocessing with Machine Learning

The first thing that we are going to take a look at here to help us get started with some of the things that we can do with machine learning is data preprocessing. You need to make sure that any data you are working with is in the right format before they can work with machine learning at all. Converting data to the right format so that you can do some work with machine learning is going to be known as data preprocessing.

Now, it is going to depend on the type of data you would like to work with, but there are going to be a few steps that need to happen to help you see the preprocessing work well. These steps are important to work with because they will ensure the data comes in the right form to be used. The steps that you should focus on for this part will include:

- Getting the data set
- Importing your libraries
- Importing the dataset
- Handling any of the missing values
- Handling the categorical data
- Dividing the data into different training sets and test sets
- Scaling the data.

Let's take a closer look at each of these and how they can work together to prepare your data the proper way.

Getting the data set

To start, all of the data sets that we are going to use in this guidebook can be found at the following link to make things easier:

https://drive.google.com/file/d/1TB0tMuLvuL0Ad1dzHRyxBX9cseOhUs_4/ view

When you get to this link, you can download the "rar" file and then copy the "Datasets" folder of to your D drive. All of the algorithms that we will use in this book will access the datasets from "D:/Datasets" folder. The dataset that you need for this chapter to help with learning more about preprocessing is known as patients.csv.

Now, we need to take a bit of time to look over this set of data. When we do that, we start to notice that there is a lot of information about the age, gender, and the BMI of the patients at hand. This set of data is also going to come with an extra column that will show us whether or not the patients we are looking over have diabetes or not. You should also notice that the age and the BMI columns are going to be numerical, while the other two columns are going to be categorical instead.

Another distinction that we need to make here is going to be between the dependent and the independent variable. When we are looking these over, the variable whose value is predicted to come in as dependent, and the variables that are used to make these predictions will become our independent variables. When we look at this kind of example, the diabetic column is going to be seen as the dependent variable because it will rely, at least a bit on the other columns there. Then we will notice that the other columns are going to be out independent options.

Importing the libraries that you need

Now that you have some of the data that you need to get started on this, you need to work on importing the library. Python automatically comes with some prebuilt libraries that can perform a variety of tasks. For this book, we are going to use the Scikit Learn Library. To keep it simple, we are going to install three libraries that are the most essential for helping us do machine learning. These include numpy, matplotlib.pyplot, and pandas.

First off is the numpy library. This is a good one to download because it can help you get some of those mathematical functions that are more complex done. Since machine learning does spend time in the mathematical field, it is worth your time to make sure that this particular library is in place.

The next library that you will want to take a look at is going to be the matplotlib.pyplot library. This is another good one that can be often used because it helps with any of the charts that you will want to work with. Often, when you are looking through some of the data that is needed to work with machine learning, it is helpful to have this library present. It at least lets you have a good idea of the data points and where they fall on the charts.

And we need to take some time to download the Pandas library. This one is important as well, and you will find that it is really easy to use. Many times a programmer is going to be able to use it to import and view any of the sets of data that they want to use with machine learning.

If you want to import these libraries, you will either need to come up with a new notebook for Python in Jupyter or you can use Spyder to open up a brand new file. The codes that we are going to focus on in this part of the guidebook are going to be useable with Spyder. To help you import these libraries, you need to work with the codes below:

```
import numpy as np
import matplotlib.pyplot as plt
import pandas as pd
```

Importing the data that you need

Once you have been able to download the three libraries that we have just talked about, it is now time to look at the steps that are needed to import the set of data that you would like to use in your chosen application. This is also going to give us a better look at why the panda's library is so important to use in this part of the process.

The data set that we are going to use will show up in the Comma Separated Values, or CSV format. The pandas library will have inside of it the read_csv function that is going to take us to the path to the SCV formatted set of data as the parameter and then will load up the set of data into the pandas data frame, which is basically going to be an object that stores the set of data in the form of rows and columns. To help us get this to happen, we need to use the code below:

```
patient_data = pd.read_csv("D:/Datasets/patients.csv")
```

The script above is going to help you to load up the data set for patients.csv in the dataset fold that you have it set. If you are using the

Jupyter notebook, this is even easier to do. You would just use the following script to help you see what the data looks like:

```
patient_data.head()
```

But, if you are working with the Spyder program, you would go over to your Variable explorer and then double click on patient_data variable from the list of variables that show up. Once you click on the right variable, you will be able to see all the details of this dataset.

When we reach this point in the process, you should then be able to see that the data frame that comes with pandas is going to look very similar to the matrix with zero-based index. Once you can load all of this up, the next step is to divide the set of data into a matrix of features and vector of dependent variables. The feature set is going to be able to hold all of the variables that you have that are considered independent.

For example, the feature matrix for patients.csv data set is going to include the information that you place for age, BMI, and gender of the patient. Also, the size that you see with your feature matrix is going to be equal to the number of independent variables by the number of records. For this example, our matrix is going to end up being three by twelve. This is because we have three independent variables and twelve patients with records we are going to look at.

To help us get started with this one, we need first to go through and create the feature. You can provide it with any name that you would like, but the traditional method of doing this is going to be with the capital X. To help us have a better chance at reading the code, we will give it the name of features, and then use the script below to make it work the way that we want.

```
features = patient_data.iloc [:,0:3].values
```

With the script that we used above, the iloc function of your data frame is used to help select all the rows as well as the first three columns from the patient_data of the data frame. This iloc function is going to take on two parameters. The first is the range of rows to select, and then the second part is going to be the range of columns you want the program to select.

If you would like to create your label vector from here, you would use the following script to get it done:

```
labels = patient_data.iloc[:3].values
```

Handling any missing values that show up

If you stop now and look at the object that is labeled patient_data, you will notice that there is a record that is missing at index 4 for the column of the BMI on that patient. To help us be able to handle it when values are missing, the easiest approach out be to find a way to remove the record that is missing a value. However, this record could also have some crucial information in it that we need to focus on, so you will sometimes want to keep it there.

Another option that you can use to help deal with some of these missing values is to add in some kind of value or character that will be able to replace the value that is missing. Often, we find that the best choice to replace that value with is either the mean or the median of all the other values that are found in that column. To help you handle the values that are missing when they come up, you just need to use the imputer class that is found in the library of sklearn.procceing. The script that you will need to make sure this happens is below

117

```
from sklearn.preprocessing import Imputer
imputer = Imputer(missing_values="Nan", strategy="mean", axis =0)
imputer = imputer.fit(features[:,1:2])
features[:,1:2] = imputer.transform(features[:,1:2])
```

With the script that we wrote above, the first line is in charge of importing the Imputer class from the right library. We then went on to create the object of the Imputer class. This is going to take on three parameters including axis, strategy, and missing_value. In terms of the missing_value parameter, we are specifying that this is the value that we want to be replaced. In our data set, the missing value is being shown by "nan". The strategy parameter is going to specify the type of strategy that we want to use to fill in this missing value. You can also choose from most-frequent, median, and mean. And then the axis parameter is going to denote which axis we want to impute here

Handling any of our categorical data

Right now we know that the algorithms that we may use with machine learning are going to be based on concepts that are mathematical in many cases, and working with these mathematics, we need to be able to work with numbers. Because of this kind of issue, it is going to become easier and more convenient for us to work in values that are categorical and then work on moving them to be numerical. When we look at the example that we are doing here, we see that two values are seen as categorical and those are the gender and diabetic options. How are we able to turn Male and Female, and Yes and No into numerical values to make things easier?

The good news is that with the sklearn. Preprocessing library, there is the LabelEncoder class, the one that is going to take your categorical column and then give you the right numerical output to make sense out of it. The script that you can use for this one includes:

```
from sklearn.preprocessing import LabelEncoder
labelencorder_features = LabelEncoder)_
features[:,2] =labelencoder_features.fit_transform(features[:,2])
```

Just like what we did with the Imputer class, the LabelEncorder class is going to have a fit_transform method, which is just a combination of the transform and the fit methods. The class is going to be able to take the categorical column that you have as the input and then will return the right numeric values to help you out.

Also, you can always take the labels vector and then convert it to a set of numeric values as follows:

```
labels = labelencoder_features.fit_transform(labels)
```

Your training sets vs. your testing sets

The next thing that we need to take a look at is the training sets and the test sets. These are going to be two very important things when it comes to the work that you are doing in machine learning, being able to separate the values that you have smartly for this to work is going to make the biggest difference overall.

Earlier on when we first introduced the idea of machine learning, we discussed that some of the models that we are looking at are going to be trained on one set of data, and then tested on a different one. This splitting up of the test and the training set is going to be done to make sure that any algorithm that you use for machine learning doesn't end up overfitting and trying too hard, messing up the data that you get. When we talk about the idea of overfitting, we are looking at the tendency that machine learning is going to do well with the results it gives on the training data, but then it ends up giving poor results when you get to the test data.

A good model that you can rely on when you work in machine learning is one that can give you some good results with both of these, with the training data and the test data. With this, we can say that the model we picked as correctly learned all of the underlying assumptions from our set of data, and then that we can accurately use it to make the decisions that we need out of any new set of data that we decide to use.

To get a better idea of how this is going to work, Let's look at the script that we use below. This script is going to help us divide up the data into the 75 percent train size, and the rest is going to be the test size.

```
from sklearn.model_selection import train_test_split
train_features, test_features, train_labels, test_labels = train_test_split
(features, labels, test_size = 0.25, random_state = 0)
```

When you execute this script above, you are going to see the train_features variable is going to contain the matrix of 9 features (because this is the 75 percent of 12) while the train_labels is going to contain the labels that correspond to this. However, with the test-features, you are going to have the remaining three features, and the test_label will have the corresponding labels.

Scaling the data we have

Now we are to the final thing that we need to look at when we get to this part of the process. We need to look at the steps that are needed to scale any of the data we have when we place it into our machine learning algorithm. It is important to know all about scaling because there are going to be some sets of data that will show up a big difference between the values that come with it.

For example, if we decided to add in a new column for the number of red blood cells of patients in this, then it is likely that the numbers are going to be hundreds of thousands (unless the patient is really sick), while it is not likely the age column would even get to 100. Many of the models that you can use with machine learning are going to use what is known as the Euclidean distance to help us find the distance that occurs in the points of data you are looking at.

The good news is that the sklearn.preprocessing library is going to contain the class known as StandardScaler that you can use to implement the standardization features. Like with other preprocessing classes, it will also contain the fit-transform that we talked about before, and it will take a data set that you provide it as the input, and then output a scaled data set. The following script will make this happen for you.

```
From sklearn.preprocessing import StandardScaler
feature_scaler = StandardScaler()
train_features = feature_scaler.fit_transform(train_features)
test_features = feature_scaler.transform(test_features)
```

One thing to note is that there isn't a need for you to scale labels on any of your classification problems. For regression problems, we will take a look at how to scale labels for a regression section.

And that is all there is to it. You need to go through some of these steps along the way to make sure that you are preprocessing the information, and that it is ready to go with the work. Your algorithms are going to be more accurate and will work out much better if you can add in these preprocessing steps to the mix. They will ensure that you can get the best results because the data is prepared in the manner that it should be.

Chapter Nine

Linear Regression with Python

Linear regression when we just have one variable

The first part of linear regression that we are going to focus on is when we just have one variable. This is going to make things a bit easier to work with and will ensure that we can get some of the basics down before we try some of the things that are a bit harder. We are going to focus on problems that have just one independent and one dependent variable on them.

To help us get started with this one, we are going to use the set of data for car_price.csv so that we can learn what the price of the care is going to be. We will have the price of the car be our dependent variable, and then the year of the car is going to be the independent variable. You can find this information in the folders for Data sets that we talked about before. To help us make a good prediction on the price of the cars, we will need to use the Scikit Learn library from Python to help us get the right algorithm for linear regression. When we have all of this setup, we need to use the following steps to help out.

Importing the right libraries

First, we need to make sure that we have the right libraries to get this going. The codes that you need to get the libraries for this section include:

```
import pandas as pd
importn numpy as np
import matplotlib.pyplot as plt
%matplotlib inline
```

You can implement this script into the Jupyter notebook The final line needs to be there if you are using the Jupyter notebook, but if you are using Spyder, you can remove the last line because it will go through and do this part without your help.

Importing the Dataset

Once the libraries have been imported using the codes that you had before, the next step is going to be importing the data sets that you want to use for this training algorithm. We are going to work with the "car_price.csv" dataset. You can execute the following script to help you get the data set in the right place:

```
car_data = pd.read_csv('D:\Datasets\car_price.csv')
```

Analyzing the data

Before you use the data to help with training, it is always best to practice and analyze the data for any scaling or any values that are missing. First, we need to take a look at the data. The head function is going to return the first five rows of the data set you want to bring up. You can use the following script to help make this one work:

```
car_data.head()
```

Also, the described function can be used to return to you all of the statistical details of the dataset.

```
car_data.describe ()
```

Finally, let's take a look to see if the linear regression algorithm is going to be suitable for this kind of task. We are going to take the data points and plot them on the graph. This will help us to see if there is a relationship between the year and the price. To see if this will work out, use the following script:

```
plt.scatter(car_data['Year'], car_data['Price'])
plt.title("Year vs Price")
plt.xlabel("Year")
plt.ylabel("Price")
plt.show()
```

When we use the script that is above, we are trying to work with a scatterplot that we can then find on the library Matplotlib. This is going to be useful because this scatter plot is going to have the year on the x-axis, and then the price is going to be over on our y-axis. From the figure for the output, we can see that when there is an increase in the year, then the price of the car is going to go up as well. This shows us the linear relationship that is present between the year and the price. This is a good way to see how this kind of algorithm can be used to solve this problem.

Going back to data pre-processing

Remember, in the last chapter, we looked at some of the steps that you need to follow to do some data preprocessing. This is done in order to help us to divide up the data and label it to get the test and the training set that we need. Now we need to use that information and have these two tasks come up for us. To divide the data into features and labels, you will need to use the script below to get it started:

```
features = car_data.iloc[:,0:1].values
labels = car+data.iloc[:,1].values
```

Since we only have two columns here, the 0th column is going to contain the feature set, and then the first column is going to contain the label. We will then be able to divide up the data so that there are 20 percent to the test set and 80 percent to the training. Use the following scripts to help you get this done:

```
from sklearn.model_selection import train_test_split
train_features, test_features, train_labels, test_labels = train_test_split
(features, labels, test_size = 0.2, random_state = 0)
```

From this part, we can go back and look at the set of data again. And when we do this, it is easy to see that there is not going to be a huge difference between the values of the years and the values of the prices. Both of these will end up being in the thousands each. What this means is that it is not really necessary for you to do any scaling because you can just use the data as you have it here. That saves you some time and effort in the long run.

How to train the algorithm and get it to make some predictions

Now it is time to do a bit of training with the algorithm and ensure that it can make the right predictions for you. This is where the LinearRegression class is going to be helpful because it has all of the labels and other training features that you need to input and train your models. This is simple to do, and you just need to work with the script below to help you to get started:

```
from sklearn.linear_model import LinearRegresison
lin-reg = LinearREgression()
lin_reg.fit (train_features, train_labels)
```

Using the same example of the car prices and the years from before, we are going to look and see what the coefficient is for only the independent variable. We need to use the following script to help us do that:

```
print(lin_reg.coef_)
```

The result of this process is going to be 204.815. This shows that for each unit change in the year, the car price is going to increase by 204.815 (at least in this example).

Once you have taken the time to train this model, the final step to use is to predict the new instance that you are going to work with. The predict method is going to be used with this kind of class to help see this happen. The method is going to take the test features that you choose and add them in as the input, and then it can predict the output that would correspond with it the best. The script that you can use to make this happen will be the following:

```
predictions = lin_reg.predict( test_features)
```

When you use this script, you will find that it is going to give us a good prediction of what we are going to see in the future. We can guess how much a car is going to be worth based on the year it is produced in the future, going off the information that we have right now. There could be some things that can change with the future, and it does seem to matter based on the features that come with the car. But this is a good way to get a look at the cars and get an average of what they cost each year, and how much they will cost in the future.

So, let's see how this would work. We now want to look at this linear regression and figure out how much a car is going to cost us in the year

2025. Maybe you would like to save up for a vehicle, and you want to estimate how much it is going to cost you by the time you save that money. You would be able to use the information that we have and add in the new year that you want it based from, and then figure out an average value for a new car in that year.

Of course, remember that this is not going to be 100 percent accurate. Inflation could change prices; the manufacturer may change some things up, and more. Sometimes the price is going to be lower, and sometimes higher. But it at least gives you a good way to predict the price of the vehicle that you have and how much it is going to cost you in the future.

This chapter spent some time looking at an example of how the linear regression algorithm is going to work if you are just working with one dependent and one independent variable. You can take this out and add in more variables if you want, using the same kinds of ideas that we discussed in this chapter as well.

Chapter Ten

Tips to Make
Machine Learning Work for You

Now that we have spent some time in this guidebook taking a look at machine learning and all of the great learning algorithms that fit into the mix, along with the different categories that come with supervised, unsupervised, and reinforcement learning, it is time to move on to putting these to use. There are so many different situations where you can utilize what you know from machine learning, and it is going to make a difference if you can work on these algorithms.

Once you have a good idea with these algorithms, you may be more curious about some of the tips and strategies that you can use to make sure that machine learning is going to work out the way that you would like. Some of the tips that you can follow when it comes to working with machine learning include:

Tip #1 Remember the Logistics

When you are working on machine learning, remember that success is not always just about picking out the right kind of algorithm or tool. It takes a bit more for this. You need to find a good fit and a good design for the specific kind of problem or project that you want to work with. Each project is going to be different, and if you try to use the same things for each one, then there are going to be situations where machine learning will not be successful.

For example, the machine learning that you use with a campaign for online marketing is going to be a lot different compared to working with an algorithm that helps guide an autonomous car. Expanding your resources for an incremental algorithm improvement is going to be worth it when it comes to the car, but in most marketing cases, you would want to optimize the different logistics around you instead.

This means that before you even get started on the project that you would like to use, you need to take some time to figure out the kind of logistics that are going to make the most sense for what you want to do. We talked about a lot of different algorithms that we can use based on the kind of project or program that you would like to focus on. And each of them presented us with something a bit different. Learning how to do these work and picking the right one for the job is important to getting the results that you want.

Tip #2 Mind the Data

Another option that we need to pay attention to is the data that you are going to put through the algorithm. One of the biggest considerations to making sure that all the algorithms you use deliver valuable insights is that you have to feed it the right kind of data. If you find that you are running data through an algorithm and the results are not coming out the way that you think they should, then it is most likely the data you are using is not right, rather than the algorithm.

There are a lot of programmers or business owners who are going to get all ego-bound and wound up, being stuck to one particular algorithm. But with all of the different tools out there, there is the possibility for way too many new algorithms. While choosing the right algorithm is indeed important to the whole process, the thing that is even more important here is making sure that you are choosing the right kind of data to help you out.

If you are studying with a harder or more complex problem like speech recognition or even something like computer vision, then that is one thing. But this field, despite what we may think when we get a bit lost in it, is that we are in a data-driven field. In most of the scenarios that we are going to find ourselves in, making some adjustments to the data that we put in rather than the algorithm is going to make a difference.

Any time that the algorithm is not providing you with the results that make sense or the results that you should be getting when you give it a try, then it is time to make some changes. Maybe you are putting in too much data, or the wrong kind of data, or even not enough data. Changing things around a bit and seeing what that does to the predictions you get may be just the change that you are looking for.

Tip #3 Algorithms Are Not Always Right

We spent a lot of time in this guidebook taking a look at the various algorithms that you can focus on. These are great tools that are going to help you to get the right results that you want, but they are not always right. If we start to look at them as magic bullets that are going to solve all of our problems instantly, then this could be a bad thing.

Implementations of machine learning are going to do their very best when there is a continual process of trial and error. No matter how good you may think the algorithms you use are if the system is doing any kind of interaction with another person, or more than one people, then it has to have some adjustments done to it over time. Businesses need always to be measuring the effectiveness of their implementation and figure out if any variables and changes are going to either make it better or make it worse.

This is going to sound like a lot of work and may seem a bit confusing when you are first getting into the field of machine learning. But it is something that you need to focus on. Very few businesses are doing this. Instead, they assume that their algorithm is perfect and that it never needs to be changed. This is going to make things worse, and over time, the algorithm is going to be so far behind that it is not going to be able to give you accurate results.

It is normal to want to deploy your system with an algorithm and then want it to do its job perfectly, without ever having to do any work to keep it that way. While that would be the ideal world, that is not a reality that any of us can count on. No algorithm or user interface design is going to be able to stick around for a long time to come. And no data collection method is going to be superseded.

That means that no matter what kind of algorithm you decide to go with, it is going to need some tune-ups and adjustments over time. If you keep up with this and don't let it fall to the side, then it is likely that the adjustments are going to be small and won't require a ton of work on your part to complete. The biggest issues are going to come when you start to ignore this step, and then the issues start to compound on each other. Remember that no algorithm, no matter how great it may seem, is going to be perfect and you do need to check on it on occasion.

Tip #4 Pick out a diverse *toolset*

As you can imagine from this guidebook and some of the other research that you may have done with machine learning, there are many different tools available to you with this field, and many of them are going to be available to you for free! This is a great thing because it allows you to have access to countless different resources available to help you get started.

But with this in mind, don't let yourself get glued to one tool. You may have one that is your favorite and that you want to use all of the time. But in reality, when you are working with machine learning, you will need to bring out several to make this successful. If there is someone around who is trying to convince you that one tool is the only one that is going to work and that you don't need any of the others, then it is time to move away from them and learn about all of the other tools that are out there.

The neat thing about machine learning is that it is growing like crazy, and some so many people are interested in learning more about it and using it for their own needs. This is good news for you because there are going to be a lot of different tools available. Experiment a few and figure out which ones are the best for you. And consider the fact that you are going to need to use a few of these to help you to get the work done.

Tip #5 Try Out Some Hybrid Learning

Another thing that you can work with is the idea of hybrid learning. You can mix some deep learning with some cheap learning to come up with a hybrid. One example of this is that you can take a vision model on a computer that is already in existence and then re-construct the top few layers, the layers that are going to contain the decision that you want to be made. From there, you can co-opt an existing framework, and then use it for a new case.

This is a great way for you to make something new, without having to create the whole thing from the very beginning. You can use some of the techniques and frameworks that are already in existence, and then add some of the specifications and more that are present in it to get the results that you would like.

This can take a bit of work. But think through some of the projects that you want to work with. Break it up into some smaller parts and figure out whether there are any existing platforms or frameworks that you can use to get things started. Once you have this, you will be able to go through and make the changes that are needed, perhaps using some of the algorithms that we already have in place and talked about above, to make this happen.

This is a benefit in many ways. First, the frameworks that you are going to be using are free in most cases or at least are not going to cost you all that much. This means that you will be able to use them and save money compared to recreating exactly what you want from scratch. It is always a good thing in business when you can save money. You still get to use the deep learning that is needed in the process, but you get the benefit of saving money on the parts that don't necessarily need to be unique.

Another benefit here is that you can save yourself some time. Many of the frameworks that you are going to use take a lot of time to create. And if you have to come up with a new one each time that you start, it is going to take forever to get projects done. When you can use or purchase the one that you would like, you can end up saving a lot of time, and it speeds along with the project that you want to get done.

Tip #6 Remember That Cheap Doesn't Mean That Something Is Bad

This is something that a lot of businesses and programmers are going to run into. We assume that when something is considered cheap or lazy that it is not going to be a good option to go with. Perhaps, you looked at the last tip and cringed a bit because you do not want to work with something that is seen as cheap because you view it as something bad.

Despite the connection that has been formed between the word cheap and being bad, this is not the case when it comes to machine learning. The amount of time that you are going to spend on one of the implementations that you want to work with machine learning is not going to necessarily correlate to the amount of value that comes to your business.

The quality that is going to be a bit more important here is to ensure that whatever process you decide to go with is reliable and repeatable. If you can achieve this in your business without having to invest too many resources or time, then this is even better. It saves you time, money, and other resources, while still providing you with a huge amount of benefit in the process.

Always remember, when it comes to machine learning that cheap doesn't mean bad. If the learning works, then it works, and it doesn't matter if it is cheap or not. You want to focus your attention on helping your customers or getting the program done, not on how much the program may have cost you along the way. If you need to spend a bit more to get the right tools or the algorithm to work, then go ahead and do it. But if you can do it for less, then why waste time and money on something that costs you more.

Tip #7 Never try to call it AI

We talked about this one a bit before. But never try to confuse AI with machine learning. Businesses need to make sure that they are using the right kind of terminology to ensure that they are getting the most out of this process. You can call these things deep learning, computer vision, or machine learning; but do not call it AI. All of these do sometimes find themselves under the umbrella of artificial intelligence as a term, but they are different.

One of the best ways that you can take a look at AI and understand it is that, right now, it is all of the things that we are not able to explain and talk about yet or the things that data scientists are not able to figure out yet. Before you have been able to figure something out, we are going to call it AI.

This is not going to be machine learning. You want to make sure that you are keeping the two apart. This will ensure that you can properly use machine learning and that you are going to get the most that you can out of these algorithms.

Tip #8 Try Out A Few Different Algorithms

With the same idea of what we talked about in terms of the different tools that are available, you also need to take some time to try out a few different algorithms. If you want to make the best decisions based on the information and the project that you are trying to work with, you want to make sure that you are working with a few algorithms. When something merges between the two, then you have a good idea that you have the best prediction for your needs.

We spent some time talking in this guidebook about some of the different types of machine learning. That means that we have a variety of algorithms that goes with each category. When you are working with the project or program that you want to create, one of the logical first steps that you should focus on is figuring out which type of machine learning you will need to make the process run smoothly.

Whether you are going to work with supervised machine learning, unsupervised machine learning, or reinforcement machine learning, it is going to direct you to the algorithms that are most likely to work for your needs. If you have no clue what kind of program or problem you need to solve, then it becomes even harder to figure out the best way to solve it and get the results that you want.

Once you have divided your particular problem up based on the type of machine learning that it is; it is time to divide things up more and figure out which algorithms are going to work the best for it. Maybe there is one learning algorithm that seems to stick out as the best choice, but try to aim for two or three if possible. This may seem like a lot of work, but it is going to make a difference in the kind of results that you can get.

First, you want to try out each of the algorithms that you choose for that set of data based on the category of machine learning that you are working with, and then you want to be able to write down the predictions or the results that you can get. If you find that some similar predictions show up between the different algorithms or the algorithms start to show one prediction that stands out from the others, and they agree on this prediction, then this is the one that you want to use for your needs.

Working with machine learning can be a really exciting time. It is going to help you to learn how to sort through some of the data sets that you have available, and it is going to make a big difference in the types of programs that you can create along the way as well. When you are just getting started with machine learning, make sure to check out this guidebook and learn some of the steps that you can take to turn this work into something that makes a world of difference in your program.

Conclusion

Indeed, Python is a very important programming language that you should learn if you are looking to be a programmer or would like to code and analyze your data. You can use Python to achieve quite a number of things; build websites, analyze statistical data, create learning algorithms and perform many other tasks of importance to you.

It is very important that you apply what you have learned here for you to retain it. One thing that I have learned over the years is that creating your own projects is a good way to push your capabilities, learn new things and build a great portfolio for your career growth.

Yes, you will get stuck a lot and hence the need for you to refer to the documentation. In that case, it is critical that you come up with more structured projects until you are comfortable to start analyzing real data using python.

That said, you have to bear in mind that python is evolving over time. This means that you have to constantly learn and work on several projects, one after the other. If you do it right, the chances are that you will look back six months ago and realize how terrible they were. If you manage to get here, then you are on the right track. You have to challenge yourself to work on projects that are uncomfortable to you, things that get you burned out and bored- that is how you learn and grow!

I wish you the very best as you learn this fun, rewarding and engaging language. With the right motivation, you will attain a high level of proficiency within a short time.

Good luck!